POLITICS, MORALITY, AND HIGHER EDUCATION

POLITICS, MORALITY, AND HIGHER EDUCATION

ESSAYS IN HONOR OF SAMUEL DUBOIS COOK

EDITED BY

F. THOMAS TROTTER

WITH CHARLES E. COLE

PROVIDENCE HOUSE PUBLISHERS

Franklin, Tennessee

Printed in the United States of America

00   99   98   97   96   5   4   3   2   1

ISBN: 1–57736–058–3

Cover by Bozeman Design

PROVIDENCE HOUSE PUBLISHERS
238 Seaboard Lane • Franklin, Tennessee 37067
800-321-5692

Contents

Contents

Preface

F. Thomas Trotter

There is a wonderful tradition in academia. When distinguished scholars retire, their colleagues present them with a volume of essays in their honor. The Germans call this a *festschrift*, which means roughly "joyous writing." It has seemed both proper and necessary to present such a volume to Samuel DuBois Cook. It is proper because he is one of the distinguished educators of our time. It is necessary because of the abiding friendships that bind these writers to their friend.

The authors share the vision of Samuel DuBois Cook that teaching and learning are moral acts, and that integrity and the search for justice are consonant with politics and political science. Thus the title of the collection: POLITICS, MORALITY, AND HIGHER EDUCATION: ESSAYS IN HONOR OF SAMUEL DUBOIS COOK. These are times when there is a pervasive skepticism about institutions. Colleges and universities are not immune. So the quality and energy of academic leadership are decisive in providing the nation with generations of young people equipped with hope and vision.

This moral urgency led Samuel DuBois Cook to leave the delights of classroom instruction at Southern University, Atlanta University, UCLA, and Illinois for the uncertainties of a university presidency. He had been an undergraduate student colleague of Martin Luther King Jr. at Morehouse College. His Ph.D. is from The Ohio State University.

The discipline of political science taught him the importance of institutions in human community. He developed insights into institutional development while at the Ford Foundation. He was the first black professor at Duke University. His leadership there was recognized when he was elected to the university board of trustees.

Cook came to the Dillard presidency in 1975. One could measure his accomplishments at Dillard by noting a 50 percent increase in the school's enrollment, a sixfold increase in its endowment, and a substantial reputation as one of the nation's premier liberal arts institutions. These are but preliminary ways of measuring his leadership.

He brought to Dillard a passion for excellence. This confident attitude permeated the entire university. He made scholarship the primary vocation of the faculty and the student body. He reminded people of his own mentor, Benjamin Mays, who taught students always to aspire to the very highest goals. Mays used to tell Morehouse students that "the cardinal sin is not low performance, mediocrity, or even failure, but low aim, the absence of high ideals." He brought to Dillard a profound religious foundation. Cook was not a denominational person. His religion was grounded in the prophetic traditions of the Bible. This gave him moral authority. It also gave him the leverage to address institutions like church and college with force and assurance. In the Council of Presidents and the University Senate of The United Methodist Church and in the United Church of Christ, he was a person of unswerving attention to the differences between the institutionally correct and the moral imperative.

He brought to Dillard an interfaith and international vision. Not content to fulfill a substantial mandate of normal expectations of a liberal arts college, Cook sought for his students a wider angle on the world. He introduced Asian studies. He linked his school with Kansei Gakuin University of Japan, and Dillard is the only historically black college with a Japanese studies program. The six-year-old National Center for Black-Jewish Relations is one of the nation's leading ongoing programs of intercultural understanding. "In the light of so many powerful common enemies, conflict and tension between blacks and Jews are simply intolerable," suggested Cook at the founding of the center.

The wider community has recognized Cook's moral leadership. He has been named to the U.S. Holocaust Memorial Council by President

Clinton. The National Conference of Christians and Jews awarded him its Weiss Award for intercultural leadership. He has also received honorary degrees from Morehouse College, The Ohio State University, Illinois College, Duke University, Chicago Theological Seminary, and the University of New Orleans.

Samuel DuBois Cook stands in the great tradition of moral leadership in the last half of the twentieth century. His speech is punctuated with quotations from four mentors who were spiritual, moral, and intellectual giants of our period. Howard Thurman taught Sam the spiritual riches of black religious faith. Reinhold Niebuhr gave him the ability to discern the moral complexities of our time. Martin Luther King Jr., his classmate, combined prophetic religion with organized social change. Benjamin Mays, whose influence continues to echo and rebound across America's intellectual landscape, gave Sam the trajectory which he followed as a university president at Dillard.

The authors to this short volume are pleased to present their contributions as a way of saying thank you to Samuel DuBois Cook, their friend and mentor, and to wish Sam and Sylvia the blessings of a happy and wondrous retirement.

Foreword

Gardner Taylor

It has been said that in the Renaissance and the Reformation, the culture of Greece rose from the dead with the New Testament in its hand. The truth of that would only prove that Dr. Samuel DuBois Cook is quintessentially a Renaissance/Reformation person.

Dr. Cook possesses a love of learning, an appreciation of the arts, a refined culture, an intellectual curiosity which combine to make him a true representative of the Renaissance epoch. At the same time, he is a profoundly religious person with a firm grasp of biblical truth. His obvious reliance on divine providence, his devotion to the great and imperishable insights of Holy Writ, and his commitment to the education of the young who are the progeny of God all indelibly mark him as a person steeped in Scripture.

As he enters a well-earned retirement, all of us who are his friends and admirers salute him and wish him Godspeed in whatever pursuits he may follow. Whatever they might be, all who hold him in esteem and affection know that he will give to them the same qualities of excellence which have marked his life. And so, as Dr. Cook lays down his responsibilities as president of Dillard University, we say to him not "hail and farewell," but rather "farewell and hail."

POLITICS, MORALITY, AND HIGHER EDUCATION

Moral Man and a Moral Journey

Hanes Walton Jr.

Born of a moral man, with a moral vision, under the tutelage of a moral leader—Benjamin Elijah Mays of Morehouse College—President Samuel DuBois Cook's moral journey was launched. In Cook's 1948 class, beside himself was none other than Martin Luther King Jr. It is no surprise then that these men were sent out by Mays on a moral journey across America's immoral landscape. It was a haunting and brooding and porous landscape, one that could seduce, lure, despoil, traumatize, and captivate the unwary, the unguarded, the unprepared, the unfocused, the unthinking, and the immoral. But these men had been sent by perhaps the most notable moral visionary of his time and generation. Mays's leadership would alter the immoral landscape at its very foundation, and with Cook and King, the unfinished task of Mays would never be the same again. Mays had prepared a second wave of moral soldiers.

King would move on to the immoral landscape via religion and conclude with a historic struggle in race relations. Cook began via political science and concluded with a historic struggle in African-American education. King would, with his "moral force," alter America's race problem forever, and Cook with his "moral intellect" reshape and remake the disciplinary problem of race and political science. In addition, he would with his "moral intellect" renew the African-American college leadership image in a moral light. Both of Mays's moral crusaders would leave their tracks and prints in the political and educational sands of time. They carried out their charge in profound, imaginative, and unexpected ways.

Both men launched their efforts in southern cities, places of old immoralities, human sins, and corruption. And in these cities and this region of the country, immorality had become an article of faith, a troubling way of life and a secular religion. This secular religion took as its chief article of faith a belief not only in the inhumanity of man to his fellow man, it taught that there could be two moralities, one for whites and another for African Americans. This secular religion gave whites a dominant place, position, and function while simultaneously placing African Americans in a lower, negative, demeaning, and inadequate spot. This secular religion gave whites dominion over African Americans. God on earth had a white skin and face. And this secular religion was ever insistent that this article of faith be accepted and believed. The unaccepting and the unwashed and the nonbelievers would suffer a life of great pain and suffering behind the veil. This secular religion had a name: segregation.

Mays challenged this secular religion with its demeaning rituals—e.g., calling white children mister, mrs., and sir—and its dehumanizing tenets and road to salvation in a segregated heaven. Mays called into question a religion based on two moralities which purported to serve the same God. Mays saw this secular religion for what it was and said so. He told Cook and King. Although this secular religion was officially called segregation, it was really white supremacy. This secular religion and political ideology were one and the same thing. And this secular religion had been institutionalized into the laws, customs, habits of society and government and thereby had created a sweeping and continuing immoral landscape. For Mays, this immoral landscape had to be confronted on its own ground and in its own place, the South. And if it was defeated in the South, where its original roots and foundations lay, the shadow and grip that it had on the rest of the nation-state would start to fade, wither, and possibly decay. Here was the charge to Cook and King. Thus, it is no surprise that they started in the South and southern cities.

In Montgomery and Atlanta, Cook and King had to confront, tackle, and overwhelm a secular religion and its immoral landscape. Cook and King had to turn a landscape, South and North, into a moral one where man's humanity to man would be accepted, and cherished and made noble. In short, their mission and crusade could be called one of justice and courage in the land of the free and the home of the brave.

King began in Montgomery, Cook in Atlanta. King began with a boycott of the bus system, Cook with lectures on the nature and promise of democracy. King called upon the masses to boycott a segregated bus system, Cook called upon the talented tenth, the rising intelligentsia, to make a new South and nation inclusive.

King preached the ignobility of the secular religion, Cook demonstrated its incompatibility with democracy and the tenets of democracy. King drew upon the African-American religion tradition to motivate and mobilize his followers against a secular religion. He told his parishioners and listeners that they would betray their own heritage by accepting and cooperating with this religion. Cook insisted to his students and colleagues that justice was not a cornerstone of the secular religion. It was a religion that combined the just (for whites only) with the unjust (for African Americans only), making it impossible for a truly democratic society. For Cook, democracy knew no such arrangement.

King called upon his followers to be nonviolent in their struggle with this secular religion and immoral landscape. Cook asked his students to attain academic excellence so that in their struggle with the secular religion they would be well-prepared. King demanded moral means for moral ends. Cook demanded the highest good for the highest achievement. King saw a beloved community. Cook envisioned a just democracy and discipline. Mays had charged them well.

King, after making his initial entrance in Montgomery, would move to carry the message and the word to Albany, Georgia; Birmingham and Selma, Alabama; Jackson, Mississippi; and Memphis, Tennessee. Needless to say, there were numerous stops in between these major cities. Cook, after making his initial entrance in Atlanta, carried the word and the message to professional conferences around the South and throughout the nation, to presidential White House meetings, and at sessions of the Southern Regional Council. King explained the shortcomings of America's democratic promise. He told all who would hear and those who would not hear that the secular religion of his day and mother's and father's past had poisoned the very spirit and soul of the democratic edifice. Cook said to a discipline that it had locked out the African-American experience and in so doing kept the discipline of political science from actually coming to grips with and grasping an understanding of the very political system and political process of which it proclaimed to render a scientific explanation. No such explanation, Cook said, could be rightfully made. The discipline had failed itself and the nation-state.

In his struggle with the immoral landscape, King found that moral suasion carried only so much influence and impact against an ensconced and entrenched secular religion. Its idols and false prophets like George Wallace refused to be easily toppled or for that matter toppled and/or dethroned by African-American moral crusaders. Wallace found backers, supporters, and true believers well beyond his native state and region. Dan Carter writes:

> For most liberals of the 1960s and 1970s, it was an article of faith that Wallace was funded by such right-wing patrons as Texas millionaire H.L. Hunt and segregationist Louisiana oilman Leander Perez, but they were mistaken. Hunt's eccentric son, Bunker, once handed over a briefcase filled with hundred-dollar bills (variously said to total $300,000 or $400,000). (Dan T. Carter, *From George Wallace to Newt Gingrich: Race in the Conservative Counterrevolution 1963–1994* [Baton Rouge: Louisiana State University Press, 1996: 10])

This was just the tip of the iceberg for the true believers, supporters and backers of this secular religion. For at times, and during certain moments in that time, state governments and federal governmental bodies supported various manifestations of this secular religion known as segregation. Dethroning it was not an easy task. Hence, King called upon the federal government itself and used it as an ally in his confrontation with the secular religion. Cook found in the discipline of political science immovable objects, ideas, theories, and models that undergirded some of the manifestations of the secular religion. Hence, Cook had to involve the Ford Foundation in supporting programs for the study of African-American politics. It was like King's effort, an ally for a breakthrough. It moved the discipline to a new epistemological plateau.

Although Mays's students—Cook and King—were transforming the immoral landscape, the storm was gathering. The secular religion was not yet finished. It was finding new allies itself and new ways to transform itself. With the conservative counterrevolution, the secular religion would be reborn. And with its born-again philosophy, this secular religion would attempt a move from the fringes and periphery of society to its center and mainstream. Here, it could repulse the most ardent and crafty assaults. But Mays had told them that immorality does not simply give up.

Therefore, King would attack not from the domestic sphere but the foreign one. King would attack the Vietnam War. It was, he said, an unjust war. And with this tactic, King moved the struggle to a new battlefield. Thus, the assault on the immoral landscape had a new battlefield. Cook moved to Duke University—a southern university steeped in the regional culture—though not always compatible with that culture. Here, Cook carried the message and the word to the sons and daughters of the very Old South. Here he would confront the emerging leaders of the New South. Here Cook was on a new battlefield. But although the battlefields had changed, the Mays vision of a just world never faded or failed to motivate these crusaders. They kept the banner flowing in the winds of change. And as before, Cook and King would be influential.

Cook's new battlefield sent a signal. To his graduate students, here was a new role, function, and base from which to struggle. The moral struggle to reshape the secular religion landscape could be fought on both fronts. It could be fought on the African-American college front and the white university front also. White universities, at least some of their students and faculties, could be enlisted in confronting the remnants of the secular religion. Hence, Cook, by example and effort, demonstrated that two battle points were better than one and with more points of confrontation, more could be done. Secondly, one of the sources of the conservative counterrevolution was in white colleges and universities. The battle points had to be moved and repositioned.

But Mays had instilled more into King and Cook than the perceptive and adroit use of battlefields. Battlefields, Mays told his young crusaders, are only signposts on the journey to the future. They are mere points on a continuum. And while these battlefields should be places of victory, they cannot become resting places. Understanding that until the secular religion is dethroned not only in its legal manifestations and in its institutional and attitudinal ones also, the struggle cannot cease with the presence of battlefields. Even more important is the fact that battlefields are but monuments to a failed past. They are not beacons of or to the future. Thus, the journey ends only with man's humanity to man.

King moved to the Poor People's March and the garbage workers' strike in Memphis. Cook moved to Dillard University. Like his mentor and patron saint, the noble Mays, Cook saw a renewed role for the private African-American college. This was Mays's legend at Morehouse. As the secular religion changes and transforms itself, a new generation of troops must be prepared to make the next assault. Given the magnificent assaults of the sixties and seventies, there were still remnants of the secular religion in society and government not only resistant but ready to renew themselves. And in this magnificent assault, King had fallen, Mays had fallen, and scores of battle-weary troops. The secular religion had exhausted a full generation of leaders, allies, organizations, and governmental backers. The coffers were empty, the resources were depleted, the ammunition was spent, and the leadership cadre was scattered. They had to be replenished, rebuilt, remade, and most importantly, recharged. There was no longer a Mays, but there was a Samuel DuBois Cook and now he was at Dillard. The new day could begin.

At Dillard, Cook became the Mays legend and he carried that legend to a new height, to a new generation, and extended moral leadership in a different sphere. Here at Dillard, Cook showed like Mays and King that man could extend humanity to his fellow man. This is the very essence of the African-American colleges. This is their role, purpose, and goal in America's society. Here lies the future. And it is here that the new dragon slayer of the secular religion is made ready and prepared for his or her next assault. Here is where the tools for the final disassembly arises. This is what Mays knew better than most. This is why he labored mightily at Morehouse. And this is the vision that he passed to Cook and King.

Here is what Cook learned. Here is the burden he assumed with the presidency of Dillard. Here is the driving force, the moving moment, the push into the millennium. It is the oppressed who must identify the sources of their oppression, prepare the assault on the secular religion, and acquire the courage to see the battle through. Cook knew that the rising intelligentsia had to be nurtured, needed to be equipped with a vision, a mission, and a sense of moral man and his or her function in an immoral landscape. An institution with a moral leadership could be tuned into this noble purpose and march with destiny. There was no other way. One could not count on the oppressor to ensure democracy for everyone. It had never happened in human history. Nor was it about to happen now, given the upsurge of the conservative counter-revolution.

Colleges and universities run by technocrats, efficiency experts, fund-raisers, and academic innovators eventually prepare students as functionaries, role models, and supporters. They prepare students to fit in, to maintain and advance the status quo. They prepare students to be peaceful revolutionaries. They prepare students not to think beyond their own specializations. Oppression, antidemocratic government, and proponents of the secular religion are expected to go away like the Model T and Model A. Progress will displace these people. Evil and the problems which evil engenders need not be confronted because enlightenment will rectify these matters. Nothing could be further from the truth. Evil is always under the sun. Secular religions have seen to it. Thus, even to envision the problem one needs at the level of higher education moral leadership.

Moral leadership, like the leadership Cook brought to Dillard, puts ethics in the center of a liberal arts education. And moral leadership makes secular religion incompatible with a college education. One cannot be fully educated and not recognize a government and society engaged in inhumanity to its own fellow citizens. One's education should not just make us good at what we do but enable us to interact and engage our fellow human beings. People are at the center of the universe. And after humankind has overwhelmed the things in the universe, people ought to be left. But without a moral compass, humankind might not be left. Here is what Cook's Dillard presidency is all about.

As Cook steps down, like Mays, the Cook presidency is about to start to play itself out against a resiliency and well-entrenched foe, one that passes itself off as a religion of the first order. A religion that insists on keeping the landscape under a spell and aura of deceit and deception. A religion insistent on a dual morality, albeit an uneven morality. It is a religion that insists on good and evil as being one and the same thing.

Cook's Dillard presidency is one that insists that morality must be a unified whole. It is a presidency that believes that man can be humane to his fellow man. It is a presidency that cries out against a landscape littered with immorality. It is a presidency that notes that in both large and small ways, unchecked immorality is corrosive of the democratic order and fabric of society. Moreover, Cook's Dillard presidency cries that justice must be about justice and only justice. It cannot embrace both justice and injustice and call the final combination justice. The masquerade must stop. Dillard men and women will confront this staggering and swaggering secular religion.

Cook's Dillard presidency has charged the troops. It has given the troops a vision, a moral armament, and a mission. The task and burden are before them. And as they embrace their charge, Cook's Dillard presidency will play itself out. The new generation will have been born. The African-American community will have heaved up another generation of warriors, a new set of talented tenth, able and willing to move the community past and beyond the revived secular religion. At this point, Cook's Dillard presidency will have achieved its final and ultimate goal. The journey will have completed itself.

But it can be said at this moment, even while the presidency moves to its final end point, that Cook's Dillard presidency has set a new standard for not only another African-American college but like the Mays presidency, for other college leaders as well. Cook's Dillard presidency says that college leadership without a moral underpinning is a sterile leadership. One that fails the students and the nation's future. Ultimately, it is a leadership that succumbs to and compromises with the secular religion and accepts the immorality of the landscape as a given and the baggage that comes with that landscape. It is immovable baggage. It is a burden that simply must be borne and worn in the daily sun and cold of the evening. It is to this thinking and doing that Cook's Dillard presidency stands against, remonstrates against, and declares immoral. It is part of the problem. Herein lies Cook's greatest contribution.

Overall, Cook's assault on the secular religion of his day and time has been a successful one. But it has also been an enduring example of what can be accomplished if one assaults the immorality of institutions, geographical regions, governments, and belief systems. For it was during this moral man's moral journey that I had the honor and privilege of meeting him and therefore myself. It was the greatest moment of my life. And because of his example, all that I am and all that I achieve, I owe to this person who became the very journey that he exemplified. He defined me, as he did so many of his Dillard students.

Congratulations on a journey well made!

2

Political Theorist, Normative Thinker, and Educational Leader

Kenneth W. Thompson

After an international relations conference in Washington in 1959, Walter Lippmann turned to a group of his colleagues and said, "I wonder how many generations it will be before we see his equal." One might have thought he was speaking of one of the full-time scholars or observers in foreign policy or international relations who were in attendance. That included James Reston, Hans J. Morgenthau, Arnold Wolfers, and George F. Kennan. However, it was Reinhold Niebuhr that Lippmann mentioned—a theologian and political philosopher, a thinker who had a profound effect on Dr. Cook.

The other towering figure in Dr. Cook's life was Dr. Benjamin Mays, who not only contributed to the intellectual and moral development of Dr. Martin Luther King Jr., but to countless others, not least Dr. Cook. Dr. Mays was a Niebuhrian in his theology and in his view of the incremental nature of progress. What Cook appropriated and made his own was an amalgam of the thought of Niebuhr and Mays. It was a union of the thought of two thinkers who were in almost every sense complementary rather than a blending of opposites. I had known Niebuhr since the late 1940s and, when I met Dr. Mays in the mid-1960s, I knew the two were kindred souls. My reaction was immediate. I could not imagine a deep gulf existing between the two, yet some of the postmodernists have tried to make the case that Niebuhr was a latecomer to civil rights. In this instance, I believe that intuition can tell us more than the behaviorists, the number crunchers, or the textual analysts who seek to explain by counting the number of times words or allusions appear in someone's article or book. I believe Dr. Cook shares my views on this subject or, more accurately, I agree with Dr. Cook.

It was no accident that Dr. Cook gravitated to political theory and thence to Niebuhr and Mays. I have not done the kind of research that would allow me to write about the young Sam Cook, but I have no doubt that, somewhere in his early background, there were factors that led to his moving in the direction of philosophy. He must have impressed his family and teachers by the workings of his inquiring mind. Philosophy, according to Max Otto, is "the great wonderment." I find it inconceivable that the young Sam Cook, whether in high school or before, did not give evidence of this trait. "The unexamined life is not worth living," philosophy tells us. Sam must have yielded to this tendency at an early age. Historians ask "what?" regarding the flow of events. Scientists are more preoccupied with "how?" By contrast, philosophers and theologians ask the question "why?" It is a question that dominates philosophical thought.

Parallel efforts manifest themselves in the study of politics, economics, law, and human relations. The impulse for a broader perspective comes from both philosophers and practitioners. Dean Acheson, secretary of state during the Truman administration, spoke often of the need for "an applicable body of theory" for politics and foreign policy. Practical men in all spheres call for more rational generalizations on their subject and intellectual structures to track the meaning of the jet stream of contemporary events. Policymakers make judgments along a moving front of events. They must do so in the face of strident debate. For a theory to be relevant, we need to sort out the intellectual factors and organize them into discrete theories.

In general, theorists deal with theory on one of three levels: history, reform, or pragmatic manipulation. History deals with the uniqueness of events. They happen once and only once. History never repeats itself exactly. A few great philosophers of history—Ranke comes to mind—use history as a check on their understanding of reality. Historical occurrences illuminate and confirm their theories. Also, theory can integrate and give direction to historical thought. In history, theory is seldom made explicit. It provides a skeleton for history, invisible to the naked eye, yet giving form and function to the body of historical events. The chronological recital of events can give content and meaning over against theoretical prepositions. History is post politics. It constitutes the raw stuff of theory. Fundamentally, however related, theory and history are not the same. Reformists, contrasted with historians, make goals and theories explicit.

Contemporary theory as such confronts the same obstacles and contradictions by which past theoretical ventures have suffered shipwreck. In economics no less than politics and human relations, theories fall short if accounting for reality. One reason is because the substance of theory is history, and history is made up of events and phenomena that are unique. Historians deal with uniqueness by concentrating on documents that provide the details that make each event unique. In this respect, history lies beyond the reach of theory. In opposition to this perspective is the assumption that the same unique events are also instances of more general propositions that explain recurrence and continuity.

Those who question the possibility of such explanatory propositions point to the variability and uniqueness of decision making. Can theories be a substitute for the art of decision making? Isn't it true that the policymaker confronts an infinite number of variables? Don't decisions involve an unending series of risky choices based on more or less rational choices? Those who defend the role of theory respond that theory can enhance the rational character of choices. It can provide the means through which decision-makers can articulate a more consistent view of the external environment. However, because the statesman is bound by the limits of contingencies and political pressures, he or she can explain actions only in terms of rough guides to action and rules of thumb. For those with a scientific bent, the condition is analogous to the medicine man in more primitive societies who became a physician with the advance of science and philosophy. The policymaker today is handicapped. He compartmentalizes decision making. He makes choices on the basis of a single experience. Cuba is a Communist state, but its dependence on Russian aid and its geographic proximity to the United States make its position unique. The answer of scientific theorists is that more data and information is capable of transforming the medicine man into "the physician of policy." Those who seek a widening of political experience rather than recourse to science are skeptical about scientific analogies. From their perspective, the realms of nature and human behavior are not equitable.

Dr. Cook shows a clear preference for political theory over science, although he has presided over a contemporary institution where it cannot be said that he was hostile to science. As a trustee of Dillard University, I know that he sought in every way to strengthen resources for science. He fought in every way possible to retain Dillard's ablest scientists. I remember instances of heroic efforts to extend the opportunities of outstanding natural scientists who happened to be critics of Dillard's programs. One of Dr. Cook's efforts was to build a strong nursing program at Dillard, a field that at the very least must be considered applied science. With some of the social science programs at Dillard, even in his own of political science, Dr. Cook consistently encouraged research endeavors that fell more at the scientific end of the discipline. His own Ph.D. program included investigations of the theories of several political theorists who recognized the importance of science. Finally, as vice-president of the American Political Science Association, Cook was conversant with the various approaches designed to advance scientific aspects of the field.

His own contribution to political thought, however, must be seen as primarily in the realm of traditional political thought. The great issues of justice and equality were never far from the center of Cook's thought. He grappled with the classical problems of morality and power going back to Aristotle and Niebuhr. Given his intellectual antecedents, rooted in Niebuhr and Mays, I would have been surprised if his emphasis had been different. The power of his analysis was as likely to come through in a report to the trustees as in a scholarly paper. As much as anyone I've known, Dr. Cook put his philosophy to work testing and re-evaluating what was true across the spectrum of human experience.

Space does not permit a comprehensive review of Dr. Cook's intellectual development—the making of a political philosopher. Suffice it to say, he pursued his graduate studies in a setting where scholarly discourse and debate were encouraged. As I remember, Professor David Spitz was his principal mentor. Earlier in his career, Spitz himself engaged in a series of lively exchanges with a disciple of Leo Strauss of the University of Chicago. Spitz was a formidable adversary and was much sought after as a spokesman for a point of view that put greater emphasis than his Straussian rival, Harry Jaffe, on the clash of contemporary philosophies. With the encouragement of Professor Spitz, Sam Cook embarked in his Ph.D. dissertation on a study of seven important political thinkers, including Niebuhr. Because of the extensive nature of his inquiry, he came to the notice of foundation officers. We were impressed by his audacity and by Professor Spitz's enthusiasm for his work. For me more was to come. I was not prepared for my introduction to Cook as potentially a major political theorist among theorists.

In the late 1950s, I attended a conference at Swarthmore College in which participants were graduate students and more serious political theorists. I sought out a panel discussion in which Cook was the principal commentator on a paper, I believe by Professor Andrew Hacker. Hacker made his presentation with characteristic flourish and brilliance. I admit to feeling pity when the chair turned to the young Cook for remarks. After a few introductory comments, I knew my concern was misplaced. Cook launched a devastating volley of criticisms, drawing not only on Hacker's paper, but also his own grasp of the history of political thought. What impressed us all was the poise and cool-headedness of the young scholar in the debate. The conference involved the cream of the crop of two groups of political philosophers: a few more senior and better-known leaders in the field and a smaller group of younger political scientists among whom Cook was clearly the standout.

After the conference, I returned to New York and made a recommendation in a form I never made before or since. I had sought Cook out and asked about his future research. He outlined some of his interests and suggested a projected study. I reported my impressions to Dean Rusk, then president of the Rockefeller Foundation. I said supporting a young scholar like Cook was something foundations had been created to do. Rusk agreed and said he would rather see support go to a few future leaders in higher education than for supplementing the already substantial endowments of a few prestigious institutions, at least one of which had a larger endowment than the foundation. Rusk suggested I call Cook requesting a project. Within the week, the whole process was complete. Looking back, I've always thought that this experience illustrated what foundations can do when an outstanding person appears on the horizon and when foundation officers trust one another. It was plain to us both that in Sam Cook's case we were in the presence of someone destined to be a leader. I was also reassured that great and highly organized institutions can move quickly when a person of highest quality such as Sam Cook appears on the scene. I found this far more satisfying as a young foundation officer than negotiating agreements with foreign governments or handling grants for large, expansive, and prestigious institutions. Much as universities, in periods of financial stringency, move toward larger and larger classes, foundations and their boards of trustees find large awards especially satisfying in the name of impact. This is true even of institutions that pay lip service to the creativity of individual scholars. What they fail to consider is the impact that an individual who early displays the mark of greatness can have on a scholarly discipline as well as on a larger segment of higher education. It was no accident that a critical reviewer of Gerald Freund's important study, *Narcissism in Philanthropy,* was a trustee of many foundations and a former president of Harvard University. Thus the story of the earliest chapter in Sam Cook's intellectual life sheds light on the need in American society for greater recognition of extraordinary talent in the midst of well-publicized institutional development.

Theories in politics are defined by the functions they serve. The first function is the ordering of data through some form of intellectual framework making possible systematic and imaginative thinking. Theories can bring order and meaning to a mass of phenomena that otherwise remain disconnected and unintelligible. They can help the observer distinguish uniformities from uniqueness. They can provide an organizing principle that defines and determines the most distinctive aspects of politics, for example, the struggle for influence and power or justice and equality. They can point to the most destructive or the most positive dimensions of a phenomenon such as politics. Theory gives the tools and the criteria whereby the observer can distinguish the recurrent from the unique. Theories must be based on certain criteria of selection of the problems for analysis. Finally, theory can be an instrument for understanding not only the uniformities and regularities but certain contingencies and irrationalities. Theory makes possible the elaboration of fruitful hypotheses bearing on the relationship between variables. If theorists deal only with similarities grounded in general principles, however, as formulated in Crane Brinton's book, *The Anatomy of Revolution*, they ignore the differences, say, between forms of violence and tyranny. Many Americans equated Nazism and Communism, yet the former was a nihilistic philosophy and the latter a utopian world view through which the most evil acts were justified by its supposedly good ends.

Distinctions are also drawn between types of political theory. Normative political theory is the study of politics in accordance with ethical desiderata. Normative thought can include the evaluation of norms as they are evolving in society. Examples of such norms are the nature of national purposes, the standards of moral discrimination, and the criteria by which we judge good and evil. Much of history teaches that humans cannot follow their interests without claiming to do so in obedience to some general scheme of values. In pursuing their ends, humans often fall victim to moral excess. Moral pretension and moral cynicism imperil moral judgment. Scholars speak of two levels of norms: first, ultimate norms that are moral standards, such as the definition of the good; and second, proximate standards that deal with factors of interest and power. Santayana provided what is perhaps the most flexible definition of the good. He wrote of the harmony of the whole which does not destroy the vitality of the parts. It is not sufficient to write of some universal concept of the good without attending to the health and vitality of the parts which make up the whole. Love is the ultimate norm, but it lies beyond history. In Berdyaev's words, "it is the norm beyond all human norms." In Augustinian terms, it represents the city of God. In the political realm, it is a transcendent norm. Nations and political parties cannot love one another. In these realms justice, not love, is the highest attainable norm. The regulative principles for justice are freedom and equality. If justice means giving each his or her due, freedom and equality are the measures of justice. A host of questions intrudes: Freedom for what? Equality in relation to what?

Political morality expresses the inevitable tension between norms and reality, between the good and the factors of interest and power. Factors which are treated as irrelevant in pure morality (the Sermon on the Mount) must be at least tentatively admitted to in the realm of social morality. Self-interest may be a source of discord ultimately but it is tentatively necessary to prevent the harmony of the whole from destroying the vitality of its parts. Power in the balance of power is a counterweight against opposing power in order to prevent injustice. Thus an alternative to chaos in some countries is tyranny, however morally ambiguous. Clearly, it is not an absolute good, but nevertheless, it may serve a moral purpose. Some societies not in a state of tyranny or chaos may be governed by custom, myth, and tradition. Thus in politics, the good is some kind of harmony, but in normative theory, the emphasis must ultimately be on precisely the kind of harmony. A good normative theory must recognize the difference between interests and ideals. The assumption in a democracy is that violence is immoral but that doesn't mean that one nation's principles which reject violence can become the contractual rules of international relations. It does allow nations to weigh the cost of one set of values against another. Normative theory calls for clarity on the objectives and purposes of society. The moral pretension regarding my nation may be a more consistent cause of conflict than competition between frankly avowed national interests.

The other type of theory is the general theory of politics and international politics. Only because history has an element of normality, regularity, and rationality can we conceive it as being susceptible to abstraction and generalization. If theorists try to be specific, they confront experiences for which general principles sometimes can't be established. Because of the uniqueness of history and the role of contingencies and accidents, general principles may apply to one case but not another. For this reason, some who discuss a general theory urge that attention be directed to middle-range theoretical problems. An example might be: "Totalitarian governments overestimate their own power and underestimate the power of others." Another might be: "Democracies are influenced by their assumption that peace is more desirable than violence."

A third form of theory involves the employment of theory as a basis for action. What are the relationships between the assumptions of statesmen and their approach to the conduct of foreign policy? What are the connections between words and deeds? What can we gain from the theoretical treatment and analysis of historic personalities and their policies? How can we trace the relation between the two? What is the relationship between the thought and action or the words and deeds of two statesmen, for example, Jefferson and Hamilton? When were their theories a guide to action and when a rhetorical or ideological tool? To what extent were their theories a basis for action and to what extent a mere ideological rationalization?

It is not difficult to determine which of these theoretical approaches captured the mind and heart of Dr. Cook. Everything we know about his philosophy and works clearly identifies him with normative theory. His mentors, to the extent they sought to generalize, did so in the context of normative thought. Niebuhr and Mays were normative theorists with few equals. Both were outside the culture that saw relevance and usefulness for the more abstract normative theories. Where the complexities and tragic dilemmas of choice were the issue, Dr. Cook and his two teachers stand in the forefront of normative thinkers.

Dr. Cook's appointment as the first African-American full professor in the social sciences at Duke University testifies to the early recognition of his work. Since an important part of his work, writings, and teaching fall in the realm of political theory, his primary commitment is clear. Moreover, it can be said that normative thinking is an integral part of his life. His theory is never divorced from practice. The two are parts of the whole. Because thought and action are inseparably linked, he has always been identified with his convictions. Dr. Cook became a full professor at Duke because of his scholarship and teaching. Without being able to prove it, I would also propose that he rose to prominence in recognition of his search for a deeper understanding of politics and morality. This was his mission. As if his scholarly recognition were not sufficient, Duke chose him as a member of its board of trustees. He has reached the pinnacle of his career as a university president and national educational leader. Every theorist or thinker must run up the flag for his particular convictions. Sam Cook chose ethics and politics or the normative theory approach.

Samuel DuBois Cook has been an educational leader in the old-fashioned way. He has been an educator as well as administrator and fund-raiser. I know few presidents of whom this can be said. More importantly, he has been able to do so because of his eminence as a political theorist and normative thinker. Obviously Sam is many other things: a devoted father, a great orator, and a loyal friend. As a vice-president at the Ford Foundation he stood out, and as a champion of equal opportunity he has few peers. From my perspective certain intellectual qualities and interests define him even more clearly. We shall all await with anticipation the fruits of his powerful and creative mind even as he remains a close and dear friend in all times and circumstances.

3

The Family, the Church, and the Historically Black College: Institutions of Achievement for the Black Community

Shirley A. R. Lewis

Dr. Samuel DuBois Cook is a virtual icon of achievement and honor for the colleges and universities historically related to The United Methodist Church. It is my pleasure and privilege to salute, praise, and thank him for his exemplary leadership in behalf of all higher education and his generous mentorship of his colleagues—the sister and brother presidents, association leaders, and denominational executives—all who aspire to serve the academically undeserved.

For me personally, this article on the impact of the church-related historically black college or university is a small way to pay tribute to this scholar-president who has exemplified extraordinary leadership as president of Dillard University for the past twenty-two years and as the executive role model exemplar for all time.

The church, the family, and the historically black colleges and universities are the three prototypic paths of achievement for the African-American community. They have served across the centuries as the significant sources of sustenance, survival, and achievement for a people bound together by a history of oppression. In this paper, these historic institutions are briefly described in terms of their strengths and needs in the hopes that these considerations may imply directions for their future health and vitality.

Frequently misdefined and poorly analyzed, the black family is nevertheless a primary institution for the African-American community.

Some appeared to limit it to perennial underachievement (Daniel P. Moynihan, *The Negro Family: The Case of National Action* [Washington, D. C.: United States Department of Labor, 1965]); others to a lack of a cultural heritage beyond the American shores (Nathan Glazer and Moynihan, *Beyond the Melting Pot* [Cambridge, Mass.: The M. I. T. Press and the Harvard University Press, 1963] and E. Franklin Frazier, *Black Bourgeoisie* [New York: Collier Books, 1962]). The black family has nevertheless served as a fount of achievement for many (Andrew Billingsley, *Black Families in White America* [Englewood Cliffs, N.J.: Prentice-Hall, 1968] and *Climbing Jacob's Ladder: The Enduring Legacy of African American Families* [New York: Simon and Schuster, 1994]; Wallace Charles Smith, *The Church in the Life of the Black Family* [Valley Forge, Penn.: Judson Press, 1985]).

Billingsley broadened black family classifications to include "nuclear" (parents and siblings), "extended" (relatives other than parents and children, and "augmented" (family head(s) not biologically related). This broadened construct is widely accepted and acknowledged in many diasporic cultures and allows scholars room to recognize certain adjuncts, e.g., informal "adoptions," gerontological services, and community role models.

Hill adds to the positive groups by identifying five common strengths of black families: (1) strong kinship bonds; (2) strong work orientation; (3) adaptability of family roles; (4) strong achievement orientation; and (5) strong religious orientation (Robert B. Hill, *The Strengths of Black Families* [New York: Emerson Hall Publishers, 1971]). Marian Wright Edelman agrees by reminding readers that in spite of difficulties, millions of black families work and have children who are graduated from high school (*Families in Peril: An Agenda for Social Change* [Cambridge, Mass.: Harvard University Press, 1987]: 7).

Billingsley shows that black families perform family functions in relatively unique ways. Whereas family theorists frequently assign instrumental functions (e.g., wage-earning) to fathers and expressive functions (e.g., nurturing) to mothers, black families may mix or exchange these functions according to circumstances. For example, black fathers experiencing unemployment may care for children and manage the household, and black mothers with greater education or wider access may be higher wage-earners (Billingsley, 1968: 23–26).

The extended family is the chief distinctive characteristic of the black family and is exemplified by extended family members' acceptance of such responsibilities as child-rearing and aiding troubled members (William H. Grier and Price M. Cobbs, *Black Rage* [New York: Bantam Books, 1968]: 871). Contrary to Moynihan's claim, black family traditions have roots which reach back to Africa. For example, the African family was also an extended family. Marriage was an elaborate process involving the immediate family, the clan, and community. Fathers played a strong role in the rearing and nurturing of children, uncles had major relationships to nieces and nephews, and bonds between brothers and sisters were exceptionally strong (Billingsley, 1968; Smith).

Slavery had a destabilizing and dehumanizing impact on the family as an institution and broke many of the established bonds of African family structure. Staples includes the splitting up of families, the prevention of black male protection of black females, the assigning of control of cabin and rations to the female, the house-slave status position, etc., as major factors of destabilization (Robert Staples, "The Myth of Black Matriarchy," in *Race Relations*, ed. Edgar G. Epps [Cambridge, Mass.: Winthrop Publishers, 1973]: 180–81). Yet remnants of the strong extended family prevailed. There are poignant accounts of freed persons traveling the South and North to reunite separated families (Paula Giddings, *When and Where I Enter: The Impact of Black Women on Race and Sex in America* [New York: William Morrow, 1984]: 57–58). The story of Ellen and Henry Craft's flight to freedom underscores a black family's devotion to the cause of freedom and to the bonds of family (Arlene Clift-Pellow, "Ellen Craft," in *Notable Black Women*, ed. Jessie Carney Smith [Detroit: Gale Research, 1992]: 239–41). Ida B. Wells's heroic battles against racial oppression are undergirded by her devotion to her husband and children. Together this family challenged racism while it raised and nurtured four children. In so doing, the Wells-Barnett family demonstrated the strength of the black family, its concern for community, and its will to survive (Linda T. Wynn, "Ida B. Wells Barnett," in *Notable Black Women*, ed. Smith).

Within the constructs of its various definitions, this institution can serve as a source of hope and revitalization. Black families frequently apply creative techniques and approaches to financial strength. Families have diversified their workforce with males providing employment and household functions, using older children as child care providers, and caring for elderly family members. The extended family character of many black families has facilitated this diversification.

Informal adoption is another example of positive black family functions. Although frequently described as "nonadoptive," black families have traditionally carried out informal adoptions by caring for, taking in, and interacting with nonrelated or distantly related children and adults. Hill states that the number of informal black adoptions continues to increase (Robert B. Hill, "Critical Issues for Black Families," in *The State of Black America* [New York: National Urban League, 1990]: 55).

Members of black families are leading efforts to improve conditions in some black communities. For example, residents in Washington, D.C., St. Louis, and New York City have led successful drives in public housing developments. The Kenilworth-Parkside tenant project in Washington, D.C., resulted in declines in crime, teen pregnancy, and school dropout and increases in the number of building repairs and rent payments (Hill, 1990: 57). In Nashville, a group of cross-generational black men established the "Nashville Sons of Africa" to work with schools, community centers, and young black males to build community and to establish an African and African-American cultural base (Ronald M. Lewis, Marcelus Brooks, and Henderson Kelly, *The Black Book of the Nashville Sons of Africa* [Nashville: Nashville Sons of Africa, 1991]).

Another strong feature of African-American families is a high achievement orientation. Family members constantly tell children, "You can do it," and "You can be what you want to be." Scholars relate the achievement orientation of black families to their heavy reliance on education as their means of success (Samuel DuBois Cook, "Black

Colleges and The United Methodist Church," *Black Issues in Higher Education*, vol. 9 [December 3, 1992]: 104; Donna L. Irwin, *The Unsung Heart of Black America* [Columbia, Mo.: University of Missouri Press, 1992]: 3; and Ronald M. Lewis, *The Selection, Retention and Later Success of Black Students at a Non-Traditional Community College* [Ph.D. diss., Stanford University, 1979]: 18–34). There are countless stories of families sacrificing in order for their children to complete high school or attend college.

The achievement legacy is a story that needs to be told in ever-widening circles. Many black family members know and rejoice in retelling the accomplishments of such extended black family members as Richard Allen, Harriet Tubman, Thurgood Marshall, Mae Jemison, Jackie Robinson, Toni Morrison, Jan Metzinger, Michael Jordan, Harry Hoosier, Althea Gibson, High John the Conqueror, Mary McLeod Bethune, Joe Louis, Louis Lomax, William A. McMillan, Leontine Kelly, Jacob Lawrence, Magic Johnson, Shirley Chisholm, Martin Luther King Jr., and Malcolm X. Black families are proud that the list of luminaries includes persons from the fields of religion, education, fine arts, social service, and science—as well as athletics!

Black families of the nineties are at risk because of a number of serious problems. Edelman's research provides chilling statistics which show that poverty is increasing among female-headed households, with black female-headed families having the greatest likelihood of remaining at the poverty level. Black children are twice as likely to die in the first year of their lives as white children. Black children are twice as likely to be unemployed as teenagers. They are three times as likely to be labeled "educationally retarded," or to be murdered between the ages of five and nine, and black children are four times as likely to be jailed as teenagers (Edelman: 3–7). We all lament the statistic that tells us that the highest rate of death for young black males is homicide (Robert L. Green, *Vital Issues Related to the Education of African American Youth*, vol. 2 [Cleveland: Center for Applied Research in Urban Education, 1991]: 19).

The African-American family faces an economic crisis. Even though the percentage of blacks with upper-class incomes has grown over the past twenty years, the income of middle-class and lower-class blacks has dropped. The percentage of families at the poverty level rose to 52 percent for black female household heads and to 14 percent for black male heads of households (Hill, 1990: 41).

The African-American community is also at risk because of teen pregnancy and nutritional problems. AIDS is reported as growing most rapidly within the African-American community (David Satcher, "Crime, Sin, or Disease: Drug Abuse and Aids in the African American Community," *Journal of Health Care of the Poor and Undeserved*, vol. 1 [fall 1990]). Stress is frequently identified as being a culturally bound illness affecting the black community. Many equate the continuing pressure of living in an institutionally racist environment as a factor in the health needs of African Americans.

Educational test scores show many blacks performing below grade level, especially after the fourth grade. Nationally, increases in black illiteracy and dropout rates are reported. Nettles's recent work shows that in spite of periodic increases, African Americans are underrepresented in colleges compared to their proportional representation in the college-age population (Frederick D. Patterson Research Institute, *African American Education: Data Book* [Fairfax, Va.: The College Fund, UNCF, 1997]: 54).

Drugs and violence dominate the quality of life for many black communities so that life, limb, and social life are affected. For many, the gang now takes the place of more traditional friendships, social clubs, and family. Crack cocaine, with its accelerated high, low price, and compelling addiction, has created a criminal behavior which many view as codeless. The result is an escalation of crime, fear, and despair in many inner cities.

Institutional racism serves to oppress blacks. Covert acts of racism continue, even in academic and secular environments, and include lack of role models, academic stereotyping, and exclusion. For many, racism appears to be alive and well and functioning unchallenged in America.

Nevertheless, there are a number of strengths which prevail for the black family. These strengths include:

1. Extended family classification: The black family is basically an extended family—one which includes relatives beyond the nuclear family, as well as selected members of the community. As such, there is a national base upon which to build positive relationships.

2. Achievement orientation: The black family is traditionally achievement-oriented, especially as this relates to high expectations for education. This tradition forms a basis for continuing positive action.

3. Strong religious commitment: Traditionally, religion plays a major role in the values and morals of the black family. A strong belief in God typically transcends the specifics of any one denomination and is frequently personalized to the life and experience of individuals and the community.

4. Legacy of survival: The black family has been ingenious in merging roles, adapting to or overcoming oppression, and forging ahead. This tenacity has brought the race through difficult times and can continue to do so.

Major problems of the black family include:

1. Appropriate definitions: The black family's strengths and contributions are frequently overlooked in conventional literature on the family. This oversight limits analysis and policy-making.

2. Increasing poverty: Increasing levels of poverty have negative impacts on the black family in the areas of family structure, school completion rates, employment, and health.

3. Diminishing health services: Diminishing economics has drastically affected health care for the poor, and undeserved black families are experiencing increased health needs at the very time that access to health care has narrowed.

4. Violence and crimes: Black families are at risk for violence and debilitating crimes, including homicide, drug offenses, and gang warfare. An additional type of violence affecting black families is police brutality.

5. Racism: Overt acts of racism, including random acts of violence and discrimination in the work place and the church, affect black families. Subtler forms of oppression bring on additional psychological pressures.

DuBois identifies the black church as the primary and revealing source of traditional black culture (W. E. B. Du Bois, *The Education of Black People* [New York: Monthly Review, 1973]). He describes the transformation of the powerful African priest into the powerful Negro preacher who served plantation slaves as interpreter and comforter. According to DuBois, the Negro church evolved from this cultural transmission into the "first distinctly Negro American social institution" (Julius Lester, ed. *The Seventh Son: The Thought and Writings of W. E. B. Du Bois*, vol. 1 [New York: Vintage Books, 1971]: 255–56).

The church has served as the primary survival institution for the black community. It is credited with being the impetus for achievement, social networking, and educational, economic, and political development (Billingsley, 1968; Hill, 1990; and Irwin). Smith claims that the sense of suffering shared by black people is a unifying feature of the black church. Felder claims that blacks view the Bible with its stories of slavery, freedom, and God's promise of a better life as relating directly to the African-American experience (Cane Hope Felder, *Troubling Biblical Waters: Race, Class and Family* [Maryknoll, N.Y.: Orbis Books, 1989]: 5). Wilmore agrees, stating, "Blacks have used religion and religious institutions as the principle expression of the people" (Gayraud S. Wilmore, *Black Religion and Black Radicalism: An Interpretation of the Religious History of Afro-American People* [Maryknoll, N.Y.: Orbis Books, 1983]: 221).

The preacher and the congregation serve as sources of uplift and promise, with the sermon and the Bible serving jointly to provide sustenance as the Word. Music, whether Negro spirituals, gospel, or "mainstream," provide interpretation and emotional uplift.

Prayer also is cited by many as a catalytic means of offering hope and salvation (Cone, 1975; Wilmore). In comparing his experiences in white and black congregations, Bowyer states, "in no other context has prayer been so clearly a means of grace as in the Black Church" (Richard O. Bowyer, "Prayer in the Black Tradition: An Overview," in *Prayer and the Black Tradition*, ed. Richard Bowyer, Betty L. Hart, and Charlotte A. Meade [Nashville: The Upper Room, 1986]: 16).

The church has also served as the catalytic response to oppression for many African Americans. Civil rights leaders, including Pastor Martin Luther King Jr. and laywoman Fannie Lou Hamer, emerged from the church to conduct liberationist training sessions (James H. Cone, *God of the Oppressed* [San Francisco: Harper and Row, 1975]; and Giddings). James Cone shows how the black church served prominently in the struggle for black liberation: "No one I knew in my Black denomination ever separated Christianity from the right to be free in society" (*Martin and Malcolm in America: A Dream or a Nightmare* [Maryknoll, N.Y.: Orbis Books, 1991]: 143).

According to Cone, Martin Luther King Jr. intentionally merged civil rights and religion into one mission. Wilmore ties the black church's role in civil rights to its nineteenth-century advocacy for the establishment of schools, political equity, social service, and African redemption. For Wilmore, the two strains of black church advocacy are the religion of survival ("make do") and the religion of liberation ("do more"). Though not absolutely divided, the two orientations are equated by Wilmore with the influence of the slave communities of the South and the influence of the free communities of the North and certain southern cities (Wilmore: 229, 231).

The black church as an instrument of liberation is reflected in Richard Allen's dramatic response to religious-racial oppression. By founding the African Methodist Episcopal Church in 1787, Allen established "one of the first national institutions concerned about the liberation and plight of all Afro-Americans" (Wilmore: 228–29). Holsey led Methodists to address the need for education by establishing Paine Institute (Othal H. Lakey, *The History of the CME Church* [Memphis:(no publisher), 1985]: 263). Cone cites Allen's protest, Henry Highland Garnet's call for freedom by any means necessary, Henry M. Turner's and Howard Thurman's association of Jesus with the

Negro, and Martin Luther King Jr.'s equation of the civil rights struggle with the gospel of Jesus as examples of the African American's response to the understanding of Scripture (Cone, 1975: 31). The responses of black United Methodists and those in the predecessor denominations follow the liberation tradition and further exemplify the role of the black church as a primary institution (James P. Brawley, *Two Centuries of Methodist Concern: Bondage, Freedom and Education of Black People* [New York: Vantage Press, 1974]).

The impact of the black church in an integrated, wider church committed to the theme of inclusivity is a very complex one. Beginning with the time of John Wesley, the black presence has served to move the white church forward along the path of justice, equality, and parity.

Black Methodists' response to the 1939 General Conference Plan of Union carried an immediate impact. Thomas reports that thirty-six out of forty-seven black delegates voted against the plan and the remaining eleven abstained. Further, when those assembled rose to sing "Marching to Zion," most of the blacks "remained seated and some of them wept" (James S. Thomas, *Methodism's Racial Dilemma* [Nashville: Abingdon Press, 1992]: 53). In the process, black Methodists provided a graphic reminder of the need for parity and justice in the church.

The all-black Central Jurisdiction advocated for parity issues within the general church. Consistent themes of concern were racial segregation within the church, the elevation and standardization of United Methodist educational institutions, the inclusion of the Liberian Annual Conference, and the abolishment of the segregated armed services (Thomas). McClain calls upon black Methodists to become more self-determining by asking themselves "whether in the grand community of United Methodism they are a saving remnant or sedimental and perhaps sentimental residue" (William B. McClain, *Black People in the Methodist Church: Whither Thou Goest?* [Cambridge, Mass.: Schenkman Publishing, 1984]: 5).

The Black (United) Methodists for Church Renewal Caucus (BMCR) was established as the conscience of the general church in its

Black Paper of 1968. This historic document, calling for educational innovations, local church support, the inclusion of black culture, and economic independence, constituted a Black Power caucus and rationale for The United Methodist Church (Black Methodists for Church Renewal Caucus, *The Black Paper: Findings of Black Methodists for Church Renewal* [Cincinnati: Black Methodists for Church Renewal, February 6–9, 1968]).

This brief review shows that the black church has functioned as a cultural and spiritual advocate and interpreter for liberationist, survivalist, moral, and social concerns and that as an institution, it is present in intraracial and interracial contexts.

The black church is an institution whose contributions overlap and interact with the black family and the historically black colleges and universities. These contributions include:

1. Sustainer: The black church has undergirded the faith, survival, and accomplishments of many African Americans.

2. Repository of black culture: African and African-American heritage is displayed and maintained through the music, rhetorical styles, behavior, and belief system of the church.

3. Catalyst for justice: The black community's strong belief in God, a personalized approach to religion, and enduring faith in humankind influence the nation and the world in terms of civil and human rights.

4. Creation of leaders: The black church has developed innumerable leaders in the religious, political, educational, and social arenas. For many African Americans, the church is the place where emerging leaders first acquire their speaking, planning, and organizing skills.

5. Liberator/survivor: Singularly or within a larger church body, the black church has served as conscience and model for harmonious relations. Black caucuses or individual pastors and laypersons have led, persuaded, or needled the wider church—or community or nation—to learn to interact with blacks and others as brothers and sisters.

6. Community service orientation: The extended family orientation often is reflected in the black church's service orientation. The traditional model includes sharing with and caring for those in the church community.

Problems within the black church institution include:

1. Underfunding: The low-giving orientation of many black churches impedes the implementation of church and community service. The low level of funding can also be a major cause for the demise of some churches.

2. Diminishing of cultural heritage: Some black churches, in the process of mainstreaming, may alter their cultural heritage traditions. In the process, the sustaining aspect of the traditional black church may be diminished or lost.

3. Uninvolvement with the at-risk community: Church programs must address at-risk populations, including the currently "unchurched." A narrowing of the gap between the middle-income and the low-income black communities is indicated.

The third institution and source of black community achievement is the historically black college or university (HBCU). Black colleges qualify as a black institution because they function as bridges to the world of achievement for African Americans and, in the case of church-related colleges, because they maintain and reflect a commitment to spiritual mission and service.

In describing the mission of the HBCUs, President Samuel DuBois Cook states: "the Black college has the same general mission as the White college, but, additionally, the Black college has a special unique purpose. . . . It is about human excellence, the superior education and training of tender minds, nourishment of the creative imagination, and reverence for learning; it is also about the development of moral character and the production of better men and women for a humane, decent and open world (Foreword, in *A Black Elite: A Profile of Graduates of UNCF Colleges*, by Daniel C. Thompson [New York: Greenwood Press, 1986]: 55).

The major thrust for private HBCUs was the church. Before Emancipation, Quakers, Methodists, and members of other denominations were prominent opponents of slavery. In 1774, John Wesley called the evil practice, "the enslavement of the noble by barbarous and inferior white men" (Brawley: 30). In 1780, Methodist annual conferences called for ministers to free their slaves and for the church to provide religious instruction. With the signing of the Emancipation Proclamation on January 1, 1863, four million black women, men, and children were released from bondage. Methodists were in the forefront of efforts to meet the educational and spiritual needs of the freedmen. For example, between 1844 and 1860, the Methodist Episcopal Church expended $1,500,000 upon Negro missions (Brawley).

As the efforts grew, more than 125 schools were established. Some evolved into colleges or universities; others were founded as such. Black and white church members, conferences, and religious groups helped form the schools. Bennett, Philander Smith, and Meharry Medical colleges were founded in the basements of Methodist churches. Paine College was founded through the cooperation of the Methodist Episcopal Church, South and the Colored (now Christian) Methodist Episcopal Church in 1882. Rust College was founded in 1866 by the Freedmen's Aid Society on a former slave auction site.

While the number of African Americans enrolled in many colleges nationally is decreasing, HBCUs are experiencing an enrollment renaissance. With their records of successful recruitment, strong retention, and outstanding graduate school and professional placements, the HBCUs continue to attract African-American and other students from across the nation. The result is outstanding; although they constitute only 3 percent of the colleges and universities in the United States, black colleges awarded 28.5 percent of the bachelor degrees earned by blacks in 1994 (The College Fund/UNCF, *UNCF* [Fairfax, Va.: UNCF, 1997]).

Wycliff states that black colleges are attracting large numbers of students from the black middle-income families as well as those in lower-income brackets. He identifies the schools' religious character as a significant part of the attraction. For Wycliff, the schools' "religious sense of mission and purpose animates students and faculty" (Don

Wycliff, "Blacks and Religious Colleges and Universities," *The Journal of the Association for Religion and Intellectual Life,* vol. 5 [summer 1988]: 20).

Many scholars have noted black parents' high expectations that their children be graduated from high school and attend college (Antoine M. Garibaldi, "Blacks in College," in *The Education of African Americans,* ed. Charles V. Willis, Antoine M. Garibaldi, and Wornie L. Reed [New York: Auburn House, 1991; and Mary R. Hoover, "Community Attitudes Toward Black English," *Language and Society,* vol. 7, 1978). Solorzano found that black students held higher educational aspirations than whites but that the gap between aspirations and attainment was wider for blacks than for whites (Daniel G. Solorzano, "An Exploratory Analysis of the Effects of Race, Class, and Gender on Student and Parent Mobility Aspirations," *The Journal of Negro Education,* vol. 61, [winter 1992]: 33).

The accomplishments of private, church-related HBCUs correlate with the high expectations expressed by black families. Thompson identifies the primary functions of HBCUs as preparing students to compete as equals in graduate schools and the professions and providing role models to inspire students to succeed (Daniel C. Thompson, *A Black Elite: A Profile of Graduates of UNCF Colleges* [New York: Greenwood Press, 1986]: 98).

For these and a variety of other reasons, black college enrollments are on the rise. Miles, Paine, and Spelman are among many schools reporting enrollment increases (Shirley A. R. Lewis, "Historically Black Colleges Enjoy a Renaissance," *Black Issues in Higher Education,* vol. 9 [August 27, 1992]; and Patterson Research Institute). Under the leadership of Dr. Samuel DuBois Cook, Dillard University's freshman class increased so significantly during each of the past several years that the university was forced to establish an enrollment cap.

The basic characteristics of HBCUs constitute the contributing factors for achievement for African Americans. The institutions' special qualities are what makes them attractive to students and parents throughout the black community.

Characteristically, HBCUs are located in traditional black communities, locations with many advantages and some disadvantages. The close proximity to the traditional community offers access to churches and service programs and, for most students, the home community. A disadvantage is that the colleges may suffer from the same problems faced by the community: deteriorating environments, increased potential for crime, and decreased public services. In nearly all cases, the college community makes great use of the advantages and works to avoid the disadvantages.

In most cases, students live in on-campus dormitories and many faculty may reside in campus housing. Generally, the president's home sits prominently on the campus. Compared to major white institutions and public historically black state colleges, private historically black colleges and universities are small. While enrollments may range from 400 to a high of 3000, the average enrollment is under 1000. The typical faculty-to-student ratio is 18:1 or lower. Students, faculty and staff know each other, both personally and intellectually.

The impact and influence of the HBCU president is a critical factor in the success of these institutions. Prominent among the names of these CEOs is that of Dr. Samuel DuBois Cook. Other frequently mentioned stellar leaders are Benjamin E. Mays (Morehouse); Johnnetta B. Cole (Spelman); and Mary McLeod Bethune (Bethune-Cookman College). The current leadership continues outstanding traditions established by their predecessors by continuing to influence students and by incorporating the high expectations model that has made these schools so successful.

The amazing record of achievements of HBCUs is great testimony to the value and need of these schools (John W. Coleman, "The Unusual Happens," *The Interpreter*, vol. 35 [February-March, 1991]; Shirley A.R. Lewis, "A Shared Dream," *The Interpreter*, vol. 32 [February-March, 1988]; and Thompson). With limited funding, underpaid faculty, and diversified student populations, the HBCUs have produced an impressive list of distinguished alumni, including Tennessee's first female surgeon, Dorothy Brown (Bennett and

Meharry); nationally acclaimed author Frank Yerby (Paine); former U.S. Surgeon General Jocelyn Elder (Philander Smith); business-woman-philanthropist Lonnear Heard (Rust); educator Marva Collins (Clark Atlanta); and bishops in the churches of the Methodist tradition: Joseph Bethea, Ernest W. Newman, and James Thomas (Claflin); W. T. Handy and Alfred Norris (Dillard); Woodie White, Marshall Gilmore, Randolph P. Shy, and Nathaniel Linsey (Paine); and Ernest T. Dixon Jr. (Huston-Tillotson); and Malawi President Hastings Kamazu Banda (Meharry). Many of the current college presidents are graduates of HBCUs including: Rust President David L. Beckley (Rust); Bethune-Cookman President Oswald P. Bronson Sr. (Bethune-Cookman); Clark Atlanta President Thomas W. Cole Jr., and Wiley President Julius S. Scott Jr. (Wiley); Alabama State University President William H. Harris (Paine); Philander Smith President Myer L. Titus (Philander Smith); Claflin President Henry N. Tisdale (Claflin); Meharry Medical President John Maupin (Meharry); and Morehouse President Walter Massey and Dillard President Samuel DuBois Cook (Morehouse).

Most HBCUs have common fiscal needs: increased endowments, physical plant maintenance and repair, increased alumni giving, grants procurement, and funds for scholarships and faculty salaries. Although their educational and general revenue base is tuition-driven, most schools are reluctant to raise tuition beyond the means of their constituency. Since most students are dependent on financial aid, each school's fiscal viability is also dependent on government aid and legislation.

Alumni giving, in most cases, is increasing. Governmental financial aid in some critical areas like Pell Grants has not increased on a par with enrollment growth. The small endowments of many schools produce relatively low revenue. The support provided by UNCF and many Christian denominations, such as the United Methodist Black College Fund, the CME church allocations, and Baptist Days, remains a critical source of support.

Many HBCUs have dual recruitment priorities: high-achieving, nationally competitive students as well as the high-potential students whose entry profiles indicate future success. Most schools accept some combination of the two categories. Both types of students have made outstanding achievements.

Though historically and predominantly African-American, black colleges and universities have a tradition of inclusiveness. The schools' charters state their openness to persons of all races and creeds. Each institution has a history which includes faculty, staff, and a small number of students from non-African-American ethnic groups. In recent years, the number of Asian, Caucasian, and Hispanic students has increased on many campuses.

The major strengths of the historically black college and universities include:

1. Strong sense of community: The colleges operate within a family-like environment. Students, faculty, and administrators know and interact with each other. The social environment prevents people from falling through the cracks and makes achievement the norm.

2. High moral and religious expectations: Because of their clear church-relatedness, the schools train students to be mission-oriented and to receive and give nurturance.

3. Achievement orientation: Students and faculty have many opportunities to achieve and to see others achieve. Thus, regardless of admissions entry profile, students in these schools know that African Americans can and should reach their goals.

4. Cultural heritage and pride: The long list of high-achieving alumni is well known to students on historically black campuses. With leaders from the African-American tradition in abundance, these schools offer a natural source of pride and inspiration.

5. Leadership training: Opportunities abound for leadership training. Through church-related activities, student government, service programs, and social and civic organizations, students obtain inspiration and practice in the area of leadership.

6. Strong friendship and social bonds: Most alumni of HBCUs are "connected" with friends they met on campus. This strong social

bond serves to unite, assist, and inspire students through their lifetimes.

Problems faced by HBCUs have a direct relationship on their future and bear special consideration and analysis.

1. Financial support: Black colleges need increased financial support from all sources. The estimated cost per student at private historically black colleges in 1991 was $7,950, compared to $14,023 for private historically white colleges (Hugh R. Fordyce and Alan H. Kirschner, *1991 Annual Statistical Report* [New York: UNCF, 1991]: 22–23]).

2. Maintenance of cultural traditions: As HBCUs continue to expand and diversify, they will respond to the need to maintain their cultural community-oriented missions. As African Americans and other students continue to flock to HBCUs, these schools will strive to maintain and value their heritage while presenting this tradition in ways which attract and benefit all students.

3. Promotion for historically black colleges: Questions continue to be asked concerning the justification for HBCUs. Some question whether these schools are still needed since historically white college and universities are now racially integrated (desegregated). Others ask whether HBCUs are as good as the historically white colleges and universities. Still others suggest that HBCUs produce graduates who will not know how to function in the predominantly white world.

Response to these concerns requires major thought and interpretation. The prevailing promotion of the contributions of HBCUs should emphasize that with comparably low resources, HBCUs produce significant numbers of graduates who function successfully in the nation and the world with dignity, grace, and expertise, and that the need for all colleges that produce African-American graduates remains critical.

The black family, the black church, and the historically black colleges and universities continue to serve as the principle sources of achievement and sustenance for the African-American community. The preservation and revitalization of these institutions are critical even as African Americans continue to move forward and to interact positively with the wider community. The future of these institutions is directly tied to the future of the African-American community. In addition, the well-being of these institutions is directly tied to the future of all Americans and to all humanity.

4

Black Studies in the Twenty-First Century: Remembering the Past, Securing the Future

William E. Nelson Jr.

Samuel DuBois Cook has influenced the lives of legions of students across the years, perhaps none more profoundly than mine. As a graduating senior at Arkansas A.M.& N. College, I was encouraged to apply to the masters program in political science at Atlanta University by one of my teachers, Professor Henry Wilkins. My major was history and government. When my major advisor, Professor Ray Russell, a historian, heard that I had applied to political science he was furious and urged that I change my graduate major to history. I wrote Atlanta University and requested that the change be made. Having heard nothing from Atlanta University by the end of the summer after my graduation, I moved to Chicago, took a probationary teaching job in the Chicago public school system, and enrolled as a part-time masters student in history at Roosevelt University. A week after I signed my contract with the Chicago public schools, I received a letter from Atlanta University that was almost returned because of insufficient postage. The letter was from Dr. Samuel DuBois Cook, offering me a Regional Fellowship in political science. This letter saved me from the wonders of history and made me a political scientist and a student of Dr. Cook. I do not know to this day what happened to my request to transfer to the history department. They say the Lord works in mysterious ways.

Since the fateful day when his letter arrived, Dr. Cook has had a commanding impact on my life. His classes at Atlanta University represented the most rewarding and productive learning experiences of my life. Sam often told us that his basic intent was to prepare us to move on to Ph.D. programs at major universities. Reeling from an incredible work load that often consisted of three term papers and twenty-five book reports, many of us believed we were being prepared too well. But, as usual, Sam knew best. When I later enrolled in the Ph.D. program at the University of Illinois, my work load dropped by 25 percent; at the same time my scholarly preparation exceeded that of fellow graduate students coming from Wisconsin, Minnesota, Michigan, and all across the Ivy League. I entered the Ph.D. program at Illinois with tremendous confidence because I knew I had been trained by one of the greatest teachers and scholars of the twentieth century. I was graduated from the University of Illinois with distinction, leaving behind Ivy Leaguers who were there long before I arrived. I was a product and a beneficiary of the Samuel DuBois Cook legacy.

I owe not only my foundation training in political science but the development of my professional career in political science to Samuel DuBois Cook. It was Dr. Cook who called Dr. Rodney Higgins, chair of political science at Southern University, to secure for me my first teaching job at Southern in 1963. When I decided to return to graduate school two years later, Dr. Cook wrote numerous letters of recommendation in my behalf. This task completed, he wrote me a letter wishing for me "an embarrassment of riches—a choice of goods." I still have that letter in my possession. Unable to make up my mind where I should attend graduate school, I called Sam and he recommended the University of Illinois—an institution where he had recently completed a visiting professorship. The universal assessment of Sam by students at Illinois when I arrived was that he was the best teacher they had ever encountered. I quickly discovered that the words "I was a student of Dr. Cook's at Atlanta University" generated instant respect from those who assumed that a black student from the South was innately unprepared for graduate work in the Big Ten. Before accepting a job at Ohio State, I again called Sam to get his advice. He informed me that

Columbus was a country town, but that Ohio State was a great university with a superior track record for recruiting and graduating black students. He highly recommended the political science department, since his great mentor David Spitz was still teaching there. After twenty-eight years of service on the faculty at Ohio State, I find that Sam's assessment remains remarkably accurate. I have enjoyed an illustrious career at The Ohio State University thanks to the talent and supreme humanity of Dr. Samuel DuBois Cook. I am honored to contribute this essay to an anthology celebrating his life and great work.

The institutionalization of black studies in decades of the 1960s represented a seminal development in the evolution of American higher education. As a historical phenomenon, black studies has deep and honorable roots. Conceptually, it is possible to trace black studies to the monumental confrontations between Africans and Europeans during the commencement of the Atlantic slave trade in the fifteenth century. Black people have always had an unquenchable thirst for knowledge. Enslaved Africans studied their environment, assessed their options, and plotted strategies designed to roll back the long curtain of racial oppression (Vincent Harding, *There Is a River: The Black Search for Freedom in America* [New York: Harcourt, Brace, Jovanovich, 1981]: 52–116).

The struggle for black liberation in America has been a political struggle. Black activists perfected the art of political struggle long before they learned formally to read and to write the English language. The language of resistance was ubiquitous. It served as the touchstone for the revolution in Haiti, guided maroon rebellions in Jamaica, served as an active ingredient in the Palmares political struggle in Brazil, and operated as a pivotal bridge linking the militant efforts of enslaved Africans in America with the storms of resistance to subjugation swirling across the Atlantic world (Eugene D. Genovese, *From Rebellion to Revolution* [New York: Vintage Books, 1979]).

Although Africans were often unlettered they were not uneducated. They studied and comprehended the intricacies of the system of racial oppression that denied to them fundamental human rights.

They cultivated a multitude of indigenous resources and used these resources to strike at the heart of the slave empire. Underground and guerrilla organizations flourished in the black community. Africans were in every sense at war with America. They organized armies, launched raids, petitioned the federal government for relief, served in the armed forces, and voted with their feet (Harding: 52–116).

It is important to understand that blacks were agents of their own liberation. Acknowledgment of black agency is very important. It means that we must rewrite the history books. A reassessment of the abolitionist movement from the perspective of black agency clearly shows that while white leaders like John Brown, William Lloyd Garrison, Wendell Phillips, and the Grimke sisters played important roles, the movement was basically carried forward on the backs of black activists such as Sarah Redmon, Charles Ray, Frederick Douglass, Sarah Forten, Robert Purvis, James McCrummell, Samuel E. Cornish, Harriet Tubman, and James McCure Smith (Benjamin Quarles, *Black Abolitionists* [London: Oxford University Press, 1969]: 3–41).

When Lincoln signed the Emancipation Proclamation he was responding, in great measure, to black agency. During the Civil War black leaders pushed for liberation, black churches rendered immensely important logistical support, the black masses dropped their farm implements and headed North. The search for effective strategies led to the founding of the Negro Convention Movement, the black emigration campaign, and the abolitionist movement. Blacks seized the ballot after the passage of the fifteenth amendment and used their legislative skills to rewrite state constitutions. Blacks served honorably in the House and Senate and captured an impressive number of state and local positions (John Hope Franklin and Alfred A. Moss, *From Slavery to Freedom*, 7th ed. [New York: McGraw-Hill, 1994]: 237–46).

Blacks joined forces with small white farmers to mount the populist campaign (Jack M. Bloom, *Race, Class and the Civil Rights Movement* [Bloomington, Ind.: Indiana University Press, 1987]: 39–46). Blacks fought tirelessly for the passage of the Blair Education

Bill and anti-lynching legislation (Harold Cruse, *Plural but Equal* [New York: William Morrow, 1987]: 10–21). The opening of the twentieth century witnessed the founding of civil rights organizations, principally by black leaders, including the Equal Rights League, the Niagara Movement, the Urban League, and the Universal Negro Improvement Association.

It is important for us to remember this history because we are still living out the legacy of that history. The basic problem remains the same: a system of white domination and black subordination remains firmly in place. Black studies came into existence to decolonize our history and politics and provide a frame of reference for the analysis of world society from an African-centered perspective (Robert Brisbane, *Black Activism* [Valley Forge, Penn.: Judson Press, 1974]: 228–37).

As an academic field, black studies can trace its origins to the polemical writings of nineteenth-century African-American historians and political activists. This period saw the emergence of detailed analyses of the black experience in America by writers such as J. W. C. Pennington, William Walker, Martin Delany, and George Washington Williams. A fundamental corps of African-American intellectuals was spawned by the establishment of the American Negro Academy in the late nineteenth century, and the flowering of research and debate within the halls of emergent black colleges and universities. The study of black history was given popular expression by Carter G. Woodson, organizer of black history week and founder of the Association for the Study of Negro Life and History. Black studies formally penetrated the mainstream of the American academy on the back of insurgency campaigns in the 1960s launched by black students and their allies (Maulana Karenga, *Introduction to Black Studies*, 2nd ed. [Los Angeles: University of Sankore Press, 1993]: 13–21). The first successful fight for black studies transpired at San Francisco State, and resulted in the appointment of Dr. Nathan Hare as the first chair of a black studies program established at a major, historically white institution (Karenga: 227–28).

Since the 1960s, black studies has evolved through three stages. The first stage was the era of political disruption. Black studies entered the academy as a political program; it was, in many respects, an extension of the civil rights movement into the sacred domain of white higher education (Karenga: 9–10). The fact should be underscored that black studies was not instituted because of white benevolence or enlightenment but because of insistent student demands. White college and university administrators charged with the responsibility of helping to establish black studies programs on campuses across the country viewed them principally as pacification programs and embraced them out of a sense of political expediency (Brisbane: 240). A number of programs disappeared quickly because as soon as the shouting stopped, administrators withdrew critical political and financial support. Many programs never received academic support and scholarly recognition. Programs that were essentially coordinating units with the bulk of their courses being taught by outside faculty found themselves in a weak position to demand and receive careful attention and extensive funding from university administrators. The programs best suited to survive were programs that were able to become free-standing academic departments and garner strong support from student and community constituents.

In the early years, black studies programs across the country faced major dilemmas. The central dilemma was the inability of programs to achieve representation inside of key university decision-making bodies. Black studies leaders quickly learned that the university was a massive bureaucratic mine field. Politics was pervasive and intense. No issues would escape the web of political wrangling. Established departments constituted a bulwark of opposition to the expansion and institutionalization of black studies. As programs evolved, they also found themselves having to grapple with problems created by faculty members who had little loyalty to black studies but merely saw black studies as a back door to regular teaching positions in the university. These individuals have contributed little to the teaching, service, and research mission of black studies; using the device of tenure as a crutch, they have become one of the biggest crosses black studies programs have had to bear.

The second period of development was the period of program consultation. This period witnessed the institutionalization of black studies in the university. A key component of this process was grudging acceptance of black studies as a permanent feature of university life by many who had originally raised strong objections to proposals for the establishment of black studies units. During the period of consolidation, the curriculum of black studies began to move towards standardization. This development was stimulated by the emergence of the National Council for Black Studies as a curriculum clearinghouse and evaluation unit.

The period of consolidation illuminated the differences between strong and weak programs. Strong programs were characterized by programmatic autonomy, an extensive core faculty, a comprehensive curriculum, and solid community support. Many weak programs were barely clinging to life, having a limited core faculty, and no base of effective operation inside or outside the university. Several strong programs were able to move to the level of graduate studies, offering M.A. degrees that focused mainly on academic subjects in the humanities and social sciences. Increasingly, black studies received stiff competition in the developmental process from women's studies and ethnic studies. This competition posed serious dangers to the fiscal viability of black studies, since university officials were more inclined to place minority studies budgets in one pot rather than expand budget allocations to meet the demands of separate minority studies programs.

A third period in the black studies development was the period of ideological conflict. This period brought into sharp relief contrasting approaches to the study of the black experience adopted by emerging groups of African-American scholars. At one end of the spectrum were the Afrocentrists, led by Molefi Asante of Temple University and author of the premier work in the field, *Afrocentricity: The Theory of Social Change* (Buffalo, N.Y.: Amulefi Publishing, 1980). At the other end were the scholarly integrationists led by Henry Louis Gates of Harvard.

The Afrocentrists believed that world society should be studied from the perspective of the African center—the values, history, ethics and interests of the African world (Karenga: 34–38). The scholarly integrationists believed that black scholarship should seek to move within the parameters of mainstream scholarship. The Gates position was given a boost by the declaration by the white media that this group represented a form of public intellect. The Asante position drew protests from white scholars who charged that the Afrocentrists were making false claims and illegitimately rewriting history. (The strongest criticism came from Mary R. Lefkowitz in her highly polemical volume, *Not Out of Africa* [New York: Basic Books, 1996].)

Another important ideological movement to emerge during this period was black women's studies. Led by Clenora Hudson Weems of the University of Missouri at Columbia and Vivian Gordon of the State University of New York at Albany, this group believed that the contributions and histories of black women deserved special analysis and structural programming (Karenga: 38–43). The drive for ideological diversity was complemented by the elevation of graduate studies in black studies at the Ph.D. level. Beginning in the early 1980s, the movement for doctoral studies would result in the establishment of fully accredited doctoral programs at the University of Massachusetts, Amherst; the University of California, Berkeley; and Temple University. While the quest for doctoral programs represented an optimistic note, by the end of the 1980s these were warning signs. Specifically, as black students began to embrace the counterculture and move away from their cultural roots, their interest in black studies as a political movement, and as a source of inspiration and enlightenment, began to decline dramatically.

As we move toward the twenty-first century, black studies faces a multiplicity of serious challenges. One challenge is the crisis of legitimacy. It is a sad commentary on the state of race relations today that after more than twenty-five years, black studies is still saddled with defending its status as a legitimate academic discipline. American higher education remains embedded in a hierarchical racial system that accords legitimacy only to those approaches to knowledge that reinforce the core beliefs and values of the white majority (Karenga: 15–21). Because teaching and research in black studies challenges the basic orthodoxy of European-centered academic approaches, questions have been frequently raised regarding the value, utility, and legitimacy of the black studies enterprise. These questions have important political ramifications, including efforts to limit the number of black studies courses, denial of departmental status to black studies programs, restrictions on funding for academic, scholarly, and administrative work in black studies, and the strict separation of black studies activities from the structure of social and political relations in the black community at large. Black studies faculty members have been the special victims of the crisis of legitimacy. These faculty members complain that their applications for tenure are judged by special standards. Frequently, the outcome of their tenure cases turns not on the excellence of their research and teaching, but the question of whether or not their academic and research interests accord with the values and orientation of mainstream, Eurocentric, educational preferences.

If the enormous potential of black studies in the twenty-first century is to be realized, we cannot continue to have black studies programs treated like alien units in the university. The challenge that black studies faces in this area is a challenge for the entire academic community. The problem of legitimacy cannot be solved unless deans, provosts, and presidents are willing to step in and use their authority to compel recalcitrant departments to do the right thing.

Black studies departments must broaden their community outreach activities. At Ohio State we are doing this through the black studies Community Extension Center. Clearly during a period in which innercity neighborhoods are experiencing severe social and economic decline, we can no longer afford the parochialism of academic elitism. Universities are powerful institutions with a vast array of resources. Black studies must lead the way in bridging the gap between the university and the community. When universities are remote from community interests, they become a part of the problem rather than a part of the solution. Public service must become the hallmark of university life in the twenty-first century.

Black studies must play a leading role in the push for social diversity on historically white college campuses. As a political as well as an academic program, black studies must be the crucial underpinning of a formidable wedge that seeks to open the doors of opportunity to minority students. And universities must do more than bring them in; they must turn them out. Black students must be given the financial support and academic counseling they need to navigate the academic process. When we provide opportunities for black students, we elevate the quality of life for all Americans. Black student recruitment is not a gift—it is an investment.

Black studies must help to prepare minority workers to meet the challenges of the twenty-first century. Researchers tell us that by 2025, minority workers will constitute the majority of the available work force. We must begin now training these workers to read, write, calculate, design, and compute. Grassroots after-school programs should become a standard component of urban-based black studies programs. No one can do this job better than those of us who are paid to cogitate, to wrestle with puzzles and find answers.

Black studies must engage in research that probes deeply into the system of values operative in today's society. We need to know why America is more concerned about draft choices in the National Football League than about thousands of babies that die every year from crack addiction and hunger. Why do we have this curious fascination with the handgun, a lethal weapon capable of killing almost nothing but a human being? How can the moral value system of a Martin Luther King Jr. or Mary McLeod Bethune help to save this society from its worst instincts? Black studies has a unique role to play in the mobilization of opinion on these issues because its perspectives are based on African value systems that stress peace and harmony with the universe. Lerone Bennett notes that it has been the special mission of black people to be the conscience of the nation. Blacks and whites live in different worlds and do not see the same reality (Lerone Bennett Jr., *The Challenge of*

Blackness [Chicago: Johnson Publishing, 1972]: 141–56). Perhaps the black vision needs to become the dominant vision. With the black vision radiating through Congress, it might be possible finally to get some serious debate started on the critical issue of gun control.

Black studies must deal with the issue of income inequality in America. Today we are seeing the upward redistribution of incomes. The rich are getting richer and the poor are getting poorer (Alphonso Pinkney, *Black Americans*, 4th ed. [Englewood Cliffs, N.J.: Prentice Hall, 1993]: 75–80).

We need to set up and fund a black studies think tank to evaluate mobile wealth and the so-called free market system. We need to know why American wealth is moving to the Pacific Rim, while workers in our communities are jobless and on the brink of starvation. We need to know why gaping loopholes exist in the tax system for corporations while average Americans are being compelled to pay more than their fair share (Claud Anderson, *Black Labor, White Wealth* [Edgewood, Md.: Duncan and Duncan Publishers, 1994]: 142–53. We must know more about an electoral process that produces politicians who care more about wringing campaign contributions from special interests than legislating ways that can repair the damage to our criminal justice system produced by our obsession with getting black men off the streets and putting them behind bars. We must know more about the connection between race and the location of toxic waste sites. We must know why Congress is inviting the worst polluters into congressional chambers to write environmental protection laws. We must know what damage is being done to our future by the wholesale abandonment of affirmative action objectives. (For a careful analysis of the affirmative action debate, see Barbara R. Bergmann, *In Defense of Affirmative Action* (New York: Basic Books, 1996].) We run the danger of losing an entire generation of minority youngsters from the talent pool. Set-aside programs that have placed blacks in business and broken the white monopoly on monopoly capitalism are disappearing at a rapid clip. Where are the economic models that forecast fiscal calamity and social disruption if we continue down the same road? Why do Britain,

Canada, and Germany have workable national health programs and we do not? Why are black women still overworked and underpaid? If we evaluate human rights by one yard stick, why is President Clinton beating a rapid path to the doorsteps of China while Nigeria remains an international pariah?

Black studies must take on these issues because there is no other academic program in the university with the values required to look beyond the hierarchical power structure of society and pose radical alternatives to the current policy agenda. Black studies is obligated to bring into existence a new world order, one in which minorities are not guests at the banquet but the innkeepers. The twenty-first century is already with us. We are a polymorphic nation with rhythms spilling into our social domain from across the world. In this environment our old-fashioned preference for racism and exclusion will not stand the test of rising expectations from below. The twenty-first century will require that we make peace with our souls and reclaim the earth for oppressed minorities. No better lessons can be taught on these subjects than the heroic campaign waged by Ida Wells Barnett against lynchings, the crusade for justice led by Paul Robeson, the appeals to collective struggles made by Marcus Garvey, and the incredible legislative accomplishments of Adam Clayton Powell, Barbara Jordan, and Shirley Chisholm.

The black studies community in the twenty-first century must be an activist community. Black studies programs cannot afford to bring on their faculties educated elites whose intellectual interests are divorced from the revolutionary strivings of the black community.

In the twenty-first century, black studies must ask new questions and offer humanizing solutions that celebrate diversity and promote maximum inclusiveness. Its objectives must not only be educational, but moral, spiritual, cultural, and political. Black progress in the twenty-first century absolutely requires that the black community uses the lessons of the past to pave the way for the realization of a more perfect future. In this process, black studies will continue to play a pivotal role.

5

The University, the Church, and Moral Leadership

F. Thomas Trotter

Colleges are tough institutions. This is especially true for small church-related institutions. Sometimes they seem to be on the very brink of disaster. Occasionally one does collapse, but most survive. When I was responsible for the more than 120 schools and colleges of The United Methodist Church, I saw several teeter on the edge. Then, to everyone's surprise, the college would find a way to continue. I called it "the Yahweh factor." That is, when all other explanations failed, one simply had to admit that God did not want that school to die.

Higher education and religion have been bound together from the beginnings of the idea of a university. The energy that created communities of learning in the Western world came from the impulse to understand and explore the created world. St. Anselm's famous definition of learning was normative: "faith seeking understanding."

The relationship between church and university has not always been a comfortable one. Clerical intervention in the investigations of scholars from time to time has been embarrassing and even frightening at times. The university has struggled over the centuries for autonomy from the church and, by the twentieth century, that struggle has been won by the academy. As Merrimon Cuninggim asserts in his last book, *Uneasy Partners: The College and the Church*, the university is no longer a junior partner nor even an equal partner.

By most accounts, the university is the senior partner in the historic relationship.

This partnership is no longer proprietary nor principally financial. But schools of learning bear in their charters and the very culture of liberal learning the maintenance of the religious traditions of the church. They carry no responsibility for theological or ideological orthodoxy but for the deep and sustaining power of the moral and ethical foundations of religion.

The independence of universities from their institutional religious ties is a fact of history. In an earlier period, Harvard's motto was "Christus Veritas." Harvard's founders were seventeenth- and eighteenth-century divines like the Mathers who measured learning by the revelation of God in Christ. Christ said, "'I am the way, the truth, and the life,'" according to St. John 14:6. In the nineteenth century, the christological element was quietly dropped and the starkly yet ambiguous motto "Veritas" survives.

Truth without a context becomes a problem. Harvard is so deeply involved in its tradition of liberal studies and theology that the university and its leadership maintain a strong presence in national leadership. But the erosion of the religious spirit in other institutions poses problems.

Alfred North Whitehead once suggested that it is more important that a proposition be interesting than that it be true. This may seem odd at first reading. But note what Whitehead is hinting. That which is self-evident may simply be "matter of fact." That which is "interesting" compels attention and response. Liberal learning is empowered by the spirit of wonder. All science has its roots in this impulse. All religion finally rests on this urgency to understand. St. Anselm's dictum continues to define intellectual work.

The communication of that urgency is the task of the university. In a world where imagination is dulled and where violence and boredom are the twin enemies of humane existence, the university offers a kind of transcendence to the culture. This is a deeply religious mission. It is religious in human terms, but not sectarian.

Reinhold Niebuhr was one of the great theological realists of this century. Many in my generation were nurtured by his religious vision of social life. He had a prophet's sense of appropriate anger and confident hope. "Nothing true or beautiful or good makes complete sense in any immediate context of history; therefore, we must be saved by faith. Nothing we do, however virtuous, can be accomplished alone; therefore, we are saved by love. Nothing worth doing is completed in our lifetime; therefore, we must be saved by hope."

In its postsectarian forms, the university lives by themes suggested by Niebuhr. The immediate context of history is an inadequate horizon for moral judgments and political strategies. So the university values the study of history as an appropriate vehicle for the forming of social and personal character. This is its faith.

The university is a community of scholars—teachers and students. The work of the university is study and research in the quest for a commonwealth characterized by moral virtue and civic participation, even the ethic of love.

The university is aware of its finitude and its incompleteness. All of the traditions of the university suggest the endless line of scholars and students, probing, pushing, and compelling data in search of understanding, well aware that succeeding generations will carry on the quest with different tools but the same hope.

To suggest such a religious structure to learning and to the university would compel some members of the university community to demur strongly. By and large, the academic community today is rather ignorant of institutional history and certainly suspicious of any form of piety. But this professional posture is unfortunately insensitive to the reality of a vast and growing religiousness in our time.

This is not denominational or institutional revival. It is, rather, a discernible hunger for meaning. It tends to be highly personal and intuitive and sometimes takes the form of fascination with non-Western traditions. It also goes by the imprecise name of "new wave" religion. This unformed reality is best characterized by its rejection of all forms of orthodoxy and institutional organization. But the phenomenon is real.

Higher education faces this reality at a time when much of it has become trivialized. Interest and wonder have been replaced by "matter of factness" and self-service. There is a vast vagueness about what is central to learning. The unity of purpose of the classical university has become fragmented. Clark Kerr once noted that the only thing that held the University of California together was the central heating system.

Faculties tend today to owe their allegiance to their professional associations rather than to their colleagues in a local faculty. Students have an understandable skepticism about the high-minded moral precepts on the college gates when they fail to notice any center to the school's moral purpose. There is a serious need for a declaration of the vocation of the university.

Presidents face that amoral landscape and look for ways to deal with it. While they wrestle with the character of young students, another issue complicates their life. This is the reality that learning has taken "industrial" forms in our period. Just when it is required for leaders to reaffirm the "religious" nature of the enterprise of learning, new challenges threaten survival.

The temptation facing university people is to be so concentrated on the survival skills that historic missions dissipate. Market issues drive academic decisions. Colleges with long and distinguished histories of liberal studies and humanistic emphases slide into entrepreneurial programs and tempting new professional programs.

Competition from aggressive distance learning and remote site enterprises is further eroding the stability of the traditional campus site institution. These imaginative enterprisers have found a formula that eliminates the costs of campus maintenance, faculty support, and student services. They use stringers as teachers, new communications technology as the classroom, and offer their programs at sharply reduced price. The net result may be the possible demise of the classical college as we have known it.

University leaders who care deeply about the vocation of the university have to give serious attention to all of these threats. At the same time, they must not lose sight of the abiding purpose of learning in the university, especially in a school that is rooted in the religious tradition.

The college or university must not only have a sense of its responsibility for the disinterested search for truth. But underlying that, there must be an articulated reason for that search. This is its sense of its vocation, its being called out with a special urgency, to the work of learning.

The church-related college is able to impose this vision in its work because, even in some truncated ways, it holds itself accountable to the traditions of Israel and the church. Obedience to that vocation is the necessary ingredient for the disinterested search for truth. The scholar, freed by trust in God, is no longer dependent upon self-esteem, professional infrastructure, or personal agenda to fulfill. Vocation is freedom. Indifference is not disinterestedness. Only a college seriously attentive to the possibility of vocation will be saved from minor and major forms of distraction.

The assignment of the university is the restoration in each generation of the moral sources of national life. Israel's vocation was iconoclastic. The prophetic tradition of Israel despised institutions that had become opaque to their purpose. Called to the destruction of opacity, the prophetic tradition declared boldly the moral authority of Yahweh.

This requires a lively sense of the need for transparent institutions. The church, the law, and the college must all be transparent in this sense. That is why they often find themselves under attack from political regimes fearful of prophetic or disinterested criticism. Our culture grants certain immunities to priests, judges, and university teachers to recognize the moral responsibilities implied in their vocations. The wearing of robes is generally restricted to these orders as a symbol of this disinterested and prophetic authority.

The university transparent to its vocation is an instrument of renewal and change in the wider society. "Be afraid to die, until you have won some victory for mankind." These words of Horace Mann are etched on his monument at Antioch College. Until recently, higher education has been based on the assumption that each generation will substantially live amid the conditions governing the lives of its parents and will transmit those conditions to mold with equal force the lives of its own children. Whitehead, writing in 1933, noted that "we are living in the first period of human history for which this assumption is false."

Think of the enormous technological changes that have taken place since 1933. Our scientific worldviews have been radically changed and are being changed even as we reflect in these pages. We have learned that American culture is not only northern European, but black and Hispanic and Asian. We have learned new languages and new music.

Our society clings desperately to the traditional and bravely limited novelty. The university has always been an innovator and society requires the energy and moral force of the university's work. All of the urgencies of our time find their feet in the university. For the church-related university, the urgency includes prophetic responsibility and moral leadership.

Now the vocation of the university needs the clarity that moral leadership requires. In our time of the collapse of other moral institutions, including government and the church, by default the assignment for a prophetic vocation resides in the university.

Whitehead suggested that the religious traditions of Israel and the church contributed the notions of foresight and novelty to our culture. The vocation of the university with religious roots is constantly to throw out a vision of the future that is shaped by the intentions of Israel and the church that a world be made new in love and justice. This is a vision that should make all of us restless with penultimate goals. The religious spirit, confident in the future, provides the wit and the will to exercise novelty in the present. Freed from the constraints of the past, empowered by a trust in the future, the present may be renewed as a fit obedience to the calling of God in the world.

The university has now to recover this obedience to its fundamental vocation to make all things new, to give new life in freedom to persons, and to challenge institutions to clarify their humane intentions. We have learned that people deprived of their own histories are easy victims of the tyrannies of the present. We have learned that the extension of freedom, justice, and hope liberates the whole community, not just those thought to be deprived.

6

The Role of the President in a Changing Context of Moral Leadership

Roger W. Ireson

In the late 1950s, a tall, sophisticated, intellectually stimulating educator was addressing a college chapel service in a United Methodist-related institution. He held the audience of students in rapt attention as he delivered an inspiring but somewhat disturbing speech. He fixed his eyes upon them as he challenged them to recognize that the person they would become was already being formed during these student days. How they would further develop and what contribution they would make was becoming irrevocably fixed through the habits and thought processes now being developed. Most students who heard the address wanted to be better than they were at that moment in time. In fact, they were on the verge of a revolution in American society but they had not sensed it yet. This man was somewhat of a prophet in the way in which he engaged student minds. He himself was an example of what a committed person could be as well as a model of what could be achieved by a keen intellect and dedicated spirit. The man was Benjamin E. Mays, president of Morehouse College, one of the great African-American educators of this century. He exemplified not only the great stature of the accomplishments of his life but also opened a window of possibility to those who encountered a towering African-American intellectual for the first time. The address was a life-transforming experience for many students, including this writer who was in the audience.

Years later I would discover that this influential African-American educator was a mentor to Samuel DuBois Cook, president of Dillard University, who followed the example of Benjamin Mays by inspiring generations of students to aspire to the best and to perform to their optimum. It is no surprise that from that class at Morehouse two great African-American leaders would emerge to shape American society and challenge a new generation to greatness. Samuel DuBois Cook was the classmate of Martin Luther King Jr. and together they would sit at the feet of their mentor and drink in his spirit and perceptive insight, which were life-transforming. Dr. Cook went on to a distinguished academic career serving both as professor and as administrator. Well known already for his contribution as a professor at Duke University, he became particularly distinguished as an effective and visionary president at Dillard University. Much could be said about his intellectual acumen and his fierce moral commitment to justice and equality. But even more special note must be made of his deep interest in and care for the lives of his students. The personal dimension has always marked the presidency of Samuel Cook, a fact to which generations of successful graduates could attest. Under his leadership, Dillard University flourished both materially and in academic excellence. Innovative educational programs combined with personal nurture in an encouraging community which produced graduates who went on to contribute to our society through exemplary accomplishments and commitment to high ideals. Anyone who has witnessed the president of Dillard sending the students forth at commencement with sage words of advice and a ringing challenge to purposeful endeavor will know that inherent in this sincere benediction was the great tradition which had once been received so many years ago at Morehouse and was being passed on to a new generation. Like his mentor before him, Samuel DuBois Cook came to epitomize the university president as a moral leader. In these pages, we pay tribute to his significant contribution to church-related higher education and we lift up the theme which so characterized his professional life, namely, the importance of moral leadership in the academic environment.

One of the more interesting discussions in an ethics class results when students are asked to define the difference between ethics and morals. It is fascinating to note the ways in which individuals have personally defined these two words so that they interact according to a definition known basically to them alone. Some will give greater emphasis to the word *morals*, while another will think that the stronger expression is found in the word *ethics*. The fact that each term has originated from a different language and basically refers to the same reality is relatively unknown to most persons. So it is that individuals invest each term with a special meaning in their understanding of the field. The word *mos* in Latin referred to a habit or a manner on the one hand or to conduct and behavior on the other hand. The plural form, *moris*, is the underlying word for what became in English morals. Cicero formed the word *moralis*, which provided the transition to the English form. The word ethics originates from the Greek word, ειωθα (eiotha), which means "to be accustomed to," and in the noun form το εθοσ (to ethos), which in its ancient Greek form referred to a stall or stable which was provided for animals. The origin of the word *ethics* then finds its meaning in providing a protected place for life to continue free from harm. Rather than meaning that those being protected were held inside with a kind of restraining enclosure, it in fact referred to holding back those forces which ravage life outside of the enclosure. So the origin of ethical codes is not to be restrictive but to provide a protected context within which life might be fulfilled without dangerous interruption or even destruction. Ethics then becomes the positive thrust of life to secure the context for attainment and fulfillment.

Perhaps one of the most creative initiatives which brought clarity to these terms was the work of Paul Lehmann. For Lehmann, morality was the actual practice or behavior which was based upon ethical foundations and enshrined in custom. Ethics, on the other hand, was reserved for behavior according to reason or a reflection upon the foundation of behavior. So the meaning of the word *ethics* points to that which holds human society together. It gives stability and security so that life can proceed. One might speak of ethics as the dynamic, thinking dimension of morals. Ethics then is a social word. One can speak of personal ethics but it is hard to determine the same without reference to the larger group or society. Religions have maintained that there is a revelatory basis for ethics which is usually enshrined in sacred scripture. In almost every case, ethical codes so revealed are the very basis for life in the community of faith. Secular sources for ethical codes can usually be found in reason alone with the highest good encompassing the goal of all behavior. Even in these systems there is a base of community in the attempt to achieve stability and fulfillment. There must always be a deeper, more penetrating reason when personal ethics as such goes against the ethical expectations of the group. Other approaches to a secular ethical system divide on the place of "duty" within the system as opposed to "purpose." Nowell-Smith in his book on ethics decries the shift from purpose and the practical to the more Kantian notion of duty as the fundamental concept of ethics. The danger of the teleological point of view in ethics becoming lost in the deontological is that the field of ethics becomes more abstract and removed from the actual lives of persons in their choices. The conceptual replaces the practical as the driving force of ethical decision making. Subsequent treatments of ethical theory have ranged over the entire spectrum briefly presented here but almost always include the sense of the importance of both the society or community and the importance of the practical nature of issues as persons struggle with the decisions of their lives. The range of ethical decisions has become more complex in the modern age as has the means of determining those things which lead to stability and fulfillment in human life.

Various approaches of determining ethical truth have been employed in both the religious and secular worlds. We have during this century gone thorough periods when an antinomian view seemed to hold sway in which no particular code seemed to guide decision making except that of a more subjective and more arbitrary choice on the part of each individual. At the other end of the spectrum were the legalists who held to a rigid moral code in their attempt to force all decision making into the categories which had been determined by previous cultures and hardened religious precepts. A new approach was fashioned by Joseph Fletcher in his attempt to break away from these extremes and to establish ethical decision making guided by the determinant of love. Fletcher urged that in each situation a person must determine what is the most loving thing to do and then make the decision accordingly. His situation ethics was an attempt to avoid a rigid objectivism with a conditioned subjectivism. Yet the implicit question of how to determine what in fact was the most loving course of action brought much criticism to this approach.

Perhaps the most enduring fusion of the use of religious insight and reason in the decision-making process was expressed by Paul Lehmann in his study, *Ethics in a Christian Context*. Finding the basis of ethical decision making in the context of community, Lehmann expressed the importance of κοινονια (koinonia), a fellowship in which, through careful deliberation informed by personal insight, reason, and religious tradition, there could be ethical determination. In the Christian context, the study of Scripture and tradition along with prayer and careful study of the issues could allow the emergence of an informed decision which could guide both the individual and the community. In this approach, one had some security without a fixed system but with the flexibility conditioned by sincere community guided by religious tradition and reason rather than individual subjectivism. While other approaches to ethical decision making arise and have their day, this koinonia approach espoused by Lehmann is the most enduring for many reasons, not the least of which is its congruence with religious tradition. Community then is at the core of ethical reflection both in terms of ultimate purpose and in regard to modus operandi of its final determination.

It is in the context of this discussion that one must consider the role of the president of a college or university as a moral leader. What it means to be a moral leader has undergone considerable interpretation and change over the last decades. The security of rigid systems has been thoroughly shattered. The temptation to respond out of frustration or even desperation has been enormous. Any sense of a sure and certain guideline has been swept away by the events and the discoveries of the last half of the twentieth century. The ability to lead out of respect born of traditional authority has disappeared on many campuses. Almost every decision is subject to challenge and not a few call forth public demonstration. Penetrating each argument is the suspicion that truth is illusive at best and contrived for personal gain at the worst. It is in such a turbulent time that men and women have had to lead our educational institutions of higher learning and seek to be moral leaders in the process. The times have called for creativity and perceptive insight from those in leadership. Perhaps during no other period has presidential moral leadership been more critical for academic institutions.

The president as a moral leader is more than ever rooted in a clear perception of community in our time. There is no longer the luxury of expounding platitudes as moral values no matter how timeless they appear to be. There is no insularity or academic "ivory tower" that will seclude the institution and its constituencies from the challenges of the modern social context. The issues polarizing society become the issues raging on the campus. In the midst of it all, there is a critical need to establish and maintain community in order that learning will continue and shared life will be possible. More than even these apparent goals, the campus as a microcosm of society calls for insight to lead the community beyond fragmentation and prejudice to a new vision of the possibilities of life together. The modern president is in a key position to provide such leadership. There is risk involved in such leadership but to do less is to fail as a moral leader. The academic institution must be guided by more than financial concerns or successful academic programs. There must be a passionate commitment to community as the heart of the institution and a vision for the future of social inter-action. The great presidents of academic institutions have been those who have understood this truth and have taken steps to implement it on their campuses. The sense of community allows learning to flourish and individual lives to be nurtured. The development of the whole person, along with academic excellence, has always been a priority for the church-related academic institution. Both goals are best achieved through community. Thus the basis for good ethical decision making is the same basis for effective academic institutions, namely, to be rooted in community both as a goal and as a social reality. In this sense, the president remains as an important moral or ethical leader in establishing the basis for effective community on the college or university campus.

The establishment of true community is one of the great challenges of the modern presidency. There have never existed more diverse groups, each with their special interest and almost unique perspective, than is now the case in the modern university. To lead with fairness and empathy is far more complex a challenge on the contemporary campus than at any previous time. The issues of gender and race are fundamental to our society and omnipresent on today's campuses. Even church-related campuses find their student body religiously diverse as well as predominantly secular in outlook. Those factors which make for a successful career are not as clearly defined as they once were, a lack of definition which creates an atmosphere of insecurity and fear in some cases. The competitive edge is now global, as is the composition of the student body. World issues have become local issues as an imperative for students no longer sequestered in one culture or political ideology. There is a tremendous need for programs which foster interaction and increased understanding. Such a program exists at Dillard University in the special seminar seeking to bring together two minority communities, the Jewish and the African-American communities, in an educational context to study together and find common sources of strength and insight in the face of prejudice and a history of injustice. The program in many of our United Methodist-related institutions in cooperation with the government of Northern Ireland which brings Protestant and Roman Catholic students from that turbulent country to our American campuses that they might be exposed to a different society as well as to modern business practices is one that intends to build and transform community. The respect and dignity which should be afforded to each individual for conscience sake rather than from the fear of litigation is a sign of moral leadership on our campuses. The president of an academic institution today is called to live out and exemplify values rather than merely espousing them. The most creative context and the most effective method to transmit those values is in the formation of community so that a campus might emerge where life and the pursuit of knowledge is protected from the ravages of destruction, a setting where there is a true ethos, a pervading understanding of the deepest shared values and respect for each individual, a setting where personal nurture and growth is the hallmark of shared life. The president of such an institution will be marked as a great moral leader. In keeping with the spirit of the dedication of this *festschrift*, Samuel DuBois Cook is such a leader.

7

A Reminiscence

Terry Sanford

Samuel DuBois Cook was a professor at Duke University when I arrived in 1969 as president, but he wasn't in town. He was on leave for special assignment in New York with the Ford Foundation, and when that assignment was complete, he had a number of other academic offers. I made it my business to see that he remained at Duke. Students liked his classes. The faculty valued his collegiality. Nationally, scholars elected him to high office in the American Political Science Association. I was pleased that I was successful in shortstopping all offers to leave Duke. I wanted him. I needed him.

Then, after a few more years of enriching our faculty and student body, Sam came to see me to report that he had received an offer from another university. "Take it!" I told him with enthusiasm. He had been offered the presidency of Dillard University. This, I knew, was a once-in-a-lifetime opportunity. For Dillard.

Sam had joined the Duke faculty in 1966 with the rank of associate professor of political science, coming from the chairmanship of political science at Atlanta University. His Ph.D. was from Ohio State, and he also had taught at Southern University and at several other universities.

He initially came to Duke as a visiting professor in 1965, at the invitation of John Hollowell, a remarkable Duke faculty member, then head of the political science department. I always figured that John had earned another star for his crown, because it was 1965, and the climate was not one clamoring for integration. John Hollowell did Duke University a tremendous service by insisting that Samuel D. Cook be given a permanent appointment at Duke. It is hard to comprehend now how that was an act of vision, and to a degree, courage, for sad to recall, there was resistance to integration even among faculty members as enlightened as those at Duke University. The old newspaper reports indicate that many in the Duke community opposed Professor Cook's admission to the faculty. Dr. Hollowell and the board of trustees of Duke prevailed, and Dr. Cook became the first African-American faculty member at Duke.

Sam took all of this, the good and the bad, with his typical sense of humor and patience and gentle understanding. He noted that he and his wife were glad to come to Duke, "in spite of the fact that everything in Durham closes at 6:00 p.m." Sam liked North Carolina, and especially the educational area in which Duke is located. He said at the time that he thought Duke was the best university in the South: "It is future-oriented, not past-oriented," he said.

The records indicate that considerable favorable correspondence about his appointment was received. Dr. Hollowell recalled one letter from an administrator of a nonsouthern university, saying, "I hear you have a black professor. Where did you find him? We want one, too."

Professor Cook also noted, "Obviously there are some bigots at Duke, but they don't bother me." And they didn't. And he quickly obtained the respect, the admiration, and the affection of the people of Duke.

While he went to Dillard, Sam Cook did not abandon Duke. He became a trustee and served the full time permitted under our bylaws. He brought a perspective, a wealth of relevant experience, and his considerable wisdom. He was, in a sense, the conscience of the board.

Of the many people in America speaking on the question of human relations, Samuel Cook speaks with considerable authority, indeed is a national spokesman. Collegiality defined Sam's presence at Duke, both as faculty member and a trustee, but that did not intrude on his determination to be forthright on sensitive issues. He was on hand to applaud the students whose famous vigil protested the failure of Duke, an exempt organization, to meet minimum-wage levels for the housekeeping and dining room employees. That was a great moment in Duke's history. The students' objections, with considerable pressure and opposition from the administration, including the calling in of local police forces, were finally resolved in favor of the position promoted by the students.

At a later time, when Sam had become a trustee, several hundred students joined hands at the point where trustees were to enter their quarterly meeting, where they would be considering divesting South African investments. Sam Cook took time to shake the hand of each student in line. Sam said this meeting, as it turned out, was one of his most significant experiences at Duke.

President Keith Brodie favored divestiture, but Sam doubted that the trustee votes were there. Here are his words, as reported at the time by the student newspaper: "I was hopeful but doubtful. I didn't think it had a chance, quite frankly. . . . I didn't think we had five votes for total divestment."

During the meeting Dr. Cook gave a short, impassioned speech in favor of divestment: "I would hate to see Duke University come down on the wrong side of a great moral issue." And he remembered, "Three or four people made comments at the right time and it just snowballed. I couldn't have been more shocked or delighted."

The vote, and Professor Cook's crucial role in it, illustrates the force of his moral vision.

Dr. Cook has done an unprecedented job as Dillard's president, building faculty quality, broadening students' opportunities, setting new records in fund-raising and endowments, establishing a new creative relationship with the city of New Orleans, adding greatly to the prestige and reputation of Dillard University.

Dillard has one of the most beautiful campuses I have seen. Dr. Cook has developed a dedicated board of trustees. He has attracted talented students. His only dereliction that I know of was his inviting me to make the commencement speech, and two times at that. It was, for me, an inspiration to visit and see his accomplishments at Dillard.

He retires now while still vigorous and will make, I am sure, additional substantial contributions to humanity.

That Sam Cook could achieve as much in America is all the more remarkable because an American man of African descent is born with prospects of not getting in the game, or if he is admitted, being dealt his cards from a stacked deck. Overcoming this tremendous American obstacle, Sam Cook set a high standard of educational excellence for himself and for his faculty, and I am sure that he has become a model for tens of thousands of students and young people in need of inspiration.

He also set an example for all of us who deplore the discrimination based on racial prejudice. As I wrote in the citation that accompanied Sam's Doctor of Laws degree, conferred by Duke University in 1979, "You have illustrated in your writings, speeches, and professional activities that a social science must be committed to the search for freedom and justice if it is to contribute fully to our civilization." Now, as then, I am proud to recognize Sam Cook's dedication to education as the liberator of minds and hearts, and to count myself fortunate to share his wisdom, his tolerance, and his friendship.

I also noted in that citation some of his successes at Duke: "We remember with pride his service to Duke University as a professor of Political Science who was selected by students for an outstanding teacher award in 1969. Your high ideals and your warm friendship awakened a response in our students that was exemplary of teaching at its best."

Sam Cook and Martin Luther King Jr. had been teenage friends, and friends throughout Dr. King's life. They were both sons of Baptist preachers. I noted that Sam, like Dr. King, had "been an ardent leader in the movement for social and racial justice and an eloquent spokesman for equality of opportunity."

Sam Cook did other things from his position as president of Dillard, in addition to raising the levels of achievement for his university. He set up at Dillard the National Center for Black-Jewish Relations. He did this because, he said, "I decided it was something I wanted to do." He received the cooperation of the Anti-Defamation League of B'nai B'rith and other civil rights organizations.

The head of the Anti-Defamation League noted that this center was playing a very positive role in the community. He noted that "Dr. Cook is a unique and wonderful human being . . . one of those old-style good people with no hidden agenda who really believes that people ought to learn how to get along . . . as sincere as he could be."

The service of Sam Cook to Duke University was celebrated in numerous ways when he retired from the board of trustees. He was presented the Duke University Medal, Duke's most significant recognition of people who have served the school, at the Founder's Day celebration in October of 1993.

I think the citation presented by President Nannerl O. Keohane ought to be preserved in full:

> This University Medalist has distinguished himself all his life. The son of a Baptist minister, he went from his hometown in Griffin, Georgia, to Morehouse College in Atlanta, earning All-Southern honors for his prowess on the football field and a Phi Beta Kappa key for his equal prowess in the classroom. He must have spent at least part of his Morehouse years sharpening the sense of justice and the love of humanity his parents instilled in him, for both he and his Morehouse friend and classmate Martin Luther King Jr. were later to become widely known and greatly revered for these qualities.
>
> From Morehouse our medalist continued his study of political science, earning his master's and doctoral degrees at Ohio State University. After two years in service to his country in the U.S. Army, he began a professional life dedicated to teaching and promoting the cause of higher education. Within a year of joining the political science faculty at Southern University, he was sought by Atlanta University to chair the department there.
>
> In 1966, Duke was successful in bringing him to join our faculty as the first African American to teach here. His classes quickly developed such a reputation that within two years the student body voted him an outstanding teacher award.
>
> A 1974 newspaper profile predicted that he was destined to lead a university; within months it came to pass when he was named

president of Dillard University. At Dillard, he quickly won praise for helping revitalize this great historically black university, both financially and intellectually, and for his unshaking commitment to equal educational opportunity and high academic standards.

Duke recognized the national significance of his achievements by awarding him an honorary doctorate of laws degree in 1979. In 1981, he was persuaded to share with us his wisdom and insight as a member of our board of trustees. From then until his election to emeritus status at the close of his term this past June, Duke University benefitted from his experience, his straightforward integrity, his gentle but steady guidance in times of moral difficulty, and the certain knowledge that he could be relied upon to remind his colleagues on the board what was the decent and moral thing to do.

This year we celebrate the 30th anniversary of the admission of the first undergraduate African-American students to Duke, and our African-American legacy more generally. It is especially fitting that this medal honors not only one of the members of our community who is personally most distinguished and accomplished, but also one who has spoken passionately and effectively across the years about the importance of a more inclusive and diverse Duke University.

And thus today, as we recall the excitement and sense of compassion he instilled in the students he taught here, the eloquence with which he has urged the university to oppose racially discriminatory practices, and the national leadership he has shown in helping promote better relations between blacks and Jews, we gratefully acknowledge the many benefits Duke has received from the selfless dedication, generous spirit and kind heart of Samuel DuBois Cook.

And so it is that Sam Cook made Duke University a better place. Sam Cook made Dillard University a better place. Wherever Sam Cook is, will be a better place.

8

Swifter Than Eagles, Stronger Than Lions

Lerone Bennett Jr.

They were swifter than eagles, they were stronger than lions.
—The Second Book of Samuel

Fifty-three years ago, Samuel DuBois Cook came out of Griffin, Georgia, unheralded and unsung, and rose to the top of one of the greatest classes of male college students ever assembled.

Martin Luther King Jr. was in that class. So were a future Harvard professor, a future editor and author, and too many future lawyers and doctors to count.

Young Samuel DuBois Cook would later dazzle them at Ohio State and Duke, but the greatest honor he ever received, save the presidency of Dillard, was the day he was elected president of a Morehouse College student body that included a disproportionately large percentage of the men who changed the temperature and the color of America in the sixties.

Young Samuel DuBois Cook arrived at a good time. In the years between 1944 and 1948, Benjamin Elijah Mays, who was perhaps the most gifted motivator of black males ever, was in residence and in his prime as president of Morehouse College, and nobody who came within sound of his voice was ever the same again. His specialty was making men out of boys and creating future leaders, college presidents, and Kings, and nobody ever did it better.

We went to Morehouse in those years maimed and marked by a system that was designed, then and now, to destroy black boys and to make them doubt themselves and their possibilities. Some of us had never seen a test tube. Some of us had never seen a library. Most of us had never seen a black man stand up straight and look a racist in the eye and call him a racist.

Mays, assisted by a band of great teachers, assisted by Chandler, Dansby, Tillman, Jones, Brisbane, Kelsey, Gloster, Williams, and Brazeal et al., accepted us where we were and put a golden crown over our heads, to use Howard Thurman's phrase, that we would spend the rest of our lives trying to grow tall enough to wear.

A black boy couldn't drink water out of white water fountains in Atlanta in that year and couldn't ride on the front seats of the bus, but Benny Mays and Company told us, in so many words, that God in his infinite wisdom had sent us to the only free oasis in this desert for black men and that as soon as we walked on that campus millions of molecules, as the late Robert E. Johnson used to say, started beating on our bodies and brains, changing our chromosomes, making it possible for us to go through the miraculous Morehouse transformation that had produced so many great black men, Mordecai Johnson, Howard Thurman, and James and Samuel Nabrit among others.

The story about the molecules was not true, strictly speaking, but believing it did Martin Luther King Jr., Robert E. Johnson, and Samuel DuBois Cook no harm, especially since it was more than a belief, especially since the transformation would not occur, Mays said, if we did not throw ourselves on the mercy of excellence, as a drowning man throws himself on a plank, and if we did not say in our heart of hearts every day and every minute of every day that no mountain was going to be too high and no ditch too deep to keep us from the sun.

They called us "Benny's Boys," all those who believed and who walked like we believed and talked like we believed. They said then that you could tell one of "Benny's Boys" a mile away, but that you couldn't tell him much.

Some of us were cited later by the president of the United States, some of us made a million dollars, one of us received the Nobel Prize, but none of us ever received a higher honor than the title, "one of Benny's Boys."

Benjamin Mays didn't teach particular classes, but he did what every great college president should do, and what few manage to do: He taught every class and every student, playing the keyboard of the campus like a great virtuoso, moving distant keys and distant strings by sympathetic vibrations. He played a particularly effective role, as is endlessly said, in changing and motivating students in his Tuesday morning chapel talks, but he was equally effective as a role model, teaching us more than is contained in all the books in all the libraries in the world by what he did as a black man fighting for freedom and truth in an unjust white world. Martin Luther King Jr.—we called him M. L. then—said later that there was a freer atmosphere on the Morehouse campus and that "for the first time in my life I realized that no one was afraid."

Can you imagine what that meant to a black boy in 1944 or, to tell the truth, in 1997? Can you imagine what it meant to M. L. King and Sam Cook?

Don't misunderstand me. Sam and M. L. and Bob and other Morehouse students didn't worship Mays, certainly not then. We argued with him, we debated him, we challenged him, and we called him—behind his back—Buck Benny, as in the Hollywood movie, *Buck Benny Rides Again*.

There were few black teachers at white universities then and the post offices of this country were filled with blacks with B.A. degrees, and yet Mays told us that if we believed in the true gospel of excellence we would go on to graduate school and get a terminal degree.

Samuel DuBois Cook believed.

We were all "Benny's Boys" in our own way, but no one believed Mays the way Sam believed him, and no one honored him more than Samuel DuBois Cook honored him.

Before taking up the Mays challenge at Ohio State and other universities, Cook met and conquered the greatest challenge of his life.

The year he was elected president of the student body—1947, if memory serves—was a year of transition at Morehouse and in the world. The great Morehouse students who had dominated the campus before the war were returning to the campus and demanding their old rights and prerogatives. One of these prerogatives was the office of president of the student body, an office that had traditionally rotated from one designated fraternity to another.

Samuel DuBois Cook was not in the loop, and the returning student leaders demanded their position, organizing a recall petition and calling a special meeting of the student body. Since they had the votes and controlled the polling machinery, it was useless for Sam to fight. The only thing he asked for was a chance to make a farewell speech to the students. The leaders of the "successful" coup agreed, making their first and final mistake.

Sam started out slowly, saying that his opponents were honorable men—"so are they all, all honorable men"—and then, without warning, he dropped a bombshell, charging that "something evil is happening here, something evil as hell!" He dragged out the words in the patented Benjamin Mays and Samuel Cook tradition, saying "eeeeeVILLLLL as heLLLLLL."

Before the leaders could catch their breath, Sam detailed a conspiracy and added that the good people of Griffin, Georgia, the people in the churches and in the fields, had sent him to Morehouse College, investing him with all their hopes and fears, and that if he failed, every black in Griffin, Georgia, failed, and that he was not going back to that little Georgia town without the title of president of the student body of Morehouse College.

When Sam got through, there was not a dry eye in the place, and the coup was over.

I was there. I heard young Sam Cook single-handedly tame a hostile crowd. I saw him walk, unscathed, out of the lion's den, and I tell you that Martin Luther King Jr. at the Lincoln Monument, Benjamin E. Mays at the World Council of Churches, and Howard Thurman in Rankin Chapel were not greater than young Sam Cook in

74

Sale Hall Chapel on that faraway day.

A man who meets himself and triumphs over himself and the world and the devil in that way is never the same again and never meets a more formidable opponent.

The Samuel DuBois Cook we know, the Samuel DuBois Cook who transformed the Dillard campus and who gave black boys and girls new hope and new confidence, was born on that day. It was that Samuel DuBois Cook, the one with a name that contains poetry and a program, who went on from triumph to triumph, becoming a distinguished political scientist and teacher. Along the way, he met and married Sylvia Fields, and they became parents of Samuel DuBois Cook Jr., a second-generation Morehouse man, and Karen Jarcelyn Cook, a second-generation Spelman woman, all of whom should be cited and noted for the record, because they are a team. The fact that they lived in the middle of the Dillard campus for twenty-two years, showing faculty members, administrators, and students what love is and what a family is, is one of the most auspicious aspects of Cook's Dillard ministry.

On January 1, 1975, Dr. Samuel DuBois Cook was installed as president of Dillard University and found his life's work. Who installed him? Who else? Benjamin Elijah Mays, proud as the father of a favorite son, proud as the teacher of a favorite student, installed him, telling him publicly not to use Dillard as a stepping-stone to other positions, saying in so many words, as he said when we left Morehouse, "Do what you do here so well that no one living, no one who ever lived, no one yet unborn could do better."

Nobody did it better, and nobody is likely to do it better. And in the doing, Dr. Cook developed his own style and gave the whole campus a new spirit, challenging and transforming black students, living and breathing excellence.

Sam and Dr. Mays and I used to call one another on Christmas Eve to say Merry Christmas. Whoever got to the phone first made the first call. I was first one year, but Sylvia told me that Sam was still at work in his office. I called Sam in his office and told him it was wrong for a father to be working that late on Christmas Eve. I next called Dr. Mays and told him that Sam was still in his office working and that I had told him that even Benjamin Mays would understand if he took Christmas Eve off. There was a long pause and then Mays said, "Ahhhhhhhhhh, I don't know about that. I'm sitting here in my office myself trying to finish the galleys on my last book." I was fifty-something on that night, but I got the message. Mays was telling me that he and Cook were keeping the faith, and that I was the only Morehouse man in the world who was not in his office and working on Christmas Eve.

Never satisfied, always pushing the envelope, always seeking the next rung on the ladder, Samuel DuBois Cook is Mays's greatest disciple, and we are indebted to him for giving a new dimension to the Mays-DuBois-Hope-Bethune-Thurman tradition in a new age and for reminding us of the great and holy time when education for black people was a total adventure and when a black with a B.A. degree was dangerous to the peace of an unjust community.

And if we are tempted to express all our love and admiration for him, it is because he has shown us all part of the hard and hardening road we must all walk together. For he ran and never got weary, defeated his enemies with their own weapons, never betrayed himself and his cause, dined with presidents and potentates and never forgot the hungry and the homeless and the humiliated. And it is an honor to salute him as he leaves a major post with honor and goes on to new mountains with honor.

Seen in historical perspective, he is one of the last lights of one of the greatest generations produced in this country. The men and women of his generation came out of the segregated Griffins of this world and turned the South and the North upside down. Samuel DuBois Cook, Martin Luther King Jr. Robert E. Johnson, Arthur Johnson, Charles Vert Willie—call the roll—were among the great lights of that generation. So were Marian Wright Edelman of Spelman, Andrew Young of Howard, Leontyne Price of Central State and, later, Jesse Jackson of North Carolina A. & T., Julian Bond, Maynard Jackson, Otis Moss,

Walter Massey, and Edwin Moses. They were, as the Bible says, swifter than eagles, and stronger than lions.

Samuel DuBois Cook was in and of that generation. He came up from Griffin, Georgia, up from segregation, up from poverty, up from denial, and he helped create the foundations of the new world of black and white America. And he is still on the case, a moral man in an immoral society, a believer in an age of nonbelievers, a long-distance runner in an age of instant coffee, instant celebrities, and instant experts. And what makes him the companion we are eager to thank and emulate is that he is still testifying, even in his leaving, telling us even as he leaves that the second greatest art is to know when to go on to a stage and that the first and greatest of all arts is to know when to leave it.

The students and the great oaks of Dillard will miss him. I for one will never forget the sight of Sam, rolling from side to side, with just a hint of a swagger in his stride, his head held high, a mist in his eyes, leading the graduation procession down the path of oaks on the Dillard campus, saying with every fiber of his being to the graduates, to the parents, to the teachers, to the whole world, "Well done."

Go tell it on the mountain, go tell it on Canal Street, and on the Mississippi River, and everywhere that Samuel DuBois Cook of Griffin, Georgia, and Dillard University kept the faith and taught us once again that the greater the obstacle the greater the triumph and the greater the glory.

9

A Legacy of Leadership

Joel L. Fleishman

As Samuel DuBois Cook relinquishes the reins of Dillard's presidency, it would be instructive, as well as appropriate, to reflect on his quarter-century of presidential leadership. Perhaps more than any president of any institution of higher education in the last half-century, Sam Cook's leadership has transformed the institution which he led. His legacy is one that not only has remarkably benefited Dillard University, but also can point the way for presidents, whether already sitting or yet to be, of other universities.

Why is leadership indispensable? Why, today, is it more difficult than ever before to exercise leadership effectively? And, finally, why is it harder to recruit principled, effective leaders for public life and all other institutions in society?

These are exciting times in which to live, times in which the pace of change is fastforwarding right before our eyes. In a flash, a micro need or niche is perceived and, faster than change has ever before occurred in history, it is filled by technologies and, frequently, by companies that hadn't existed before the need or niche was noticed.

It is an exciting time, too, because of the speedup in the evolution of macro changes in the world. We are living in an era in which, for all of its fits and starts, for all of its violence and bloodshed, for all of the racial, ethnic and religious hatreds that persist, and break our hearts, the globe—and yes, it is ever more clearly being seen to be a global village, as Marshall McLuhan predicted—is headed in the right direction, the direction of expanding human freedom, loosening the bonds of the oppressed, and greater self-direction for individuals, business organizations, voluntary associations, and nations alike. With the collapse of Communism in Russia and Eastern Europe, the transformation of South Africa into a multiracial democracy, the seemingly relentless march of freer commercial, intellectual and political market systems all across the globe, and the corresponding retreat of statist practices everywhere, the shackles of oppression are being cast off and the energies of individuals and communities are being set free to "burgeon out all that is within them," as Thomas Wolfe once wrote.

We are witnessing the ever-more pervasive social blossoming of brilliant insights that first sprouted from the genius of Adam Smith, a professor of moral philosophy at the University of Glasgow in Scotland, some two hundred and fifty years ago, during what has now come to be known as the Scottish Enlightenment. In the economic gloom of backward Scotland, Smith's imagination sparked a flame that is now beginning to banish all kinds of darkness everywhere—the darkness of poverty, of command economies, of authoritarian governments, of brutal repression of human rights and liberties, of muzzled speech, of arbitrariness, of force and power and politics as the only matters that count. Adam Smith's spark, which his writings fanned into a bit of a flame even during his lifetime, set free the competitive play of ideas and ideals in the world, of such ideas as free markets, free trade, free politics, free speech, free societies, free associations, and, yes, free human beings. He understood, perhaps more clearly than any thinker before or since, that, if a free play of human ideas and initiatives exists, no social and economic darkness is ever truly dark. And if such a free play grows vigorous, no society will remain dark for very long. And that is Smith's truly original invention—the voluntary society only lightly regulated by the heavy hand of government.

In retrospect, we see clearly now that what is centrally wrong about command societies is their practice, by definition, of restraining, indeed suppressing, individual initiative and expression. The consequence is an entire society shaped by the vision and will of those doing the commanding, and, no matter how noble its intentions, it must fail because it is closed to the expression of the ideas of any others than those doing the commanding. Even if such a society is essentially good in the beginning, its energies quickly flag because it has no source of refreshment independent of those controlling it. And if it is bad, as it usually is, it creates a horror utterly unrelieved by any good. What makes life endurable today in our own society, with all the violence and hatred we encounter so frequently, is the fact that there is so much good happening at the same time that we can realistically hope that things will get better. Command societies permit no such hope because they suppress the independent sources of life-refreshing good. As John Stuart Mill, writing in the nineteenth century, noted: "Not the violent conflict between parts of the truth, but the quiet suppression of half of it, is the formidable evil; there is always hope when people are forced to listen to both sides."

While the brilliant Adam Smith is best known for his pioneering work on economics, *The Wealth of Nations*, in which his empirical research buttressed his argument for the superiority of free trade between nations and free economic activity within nations, the truth is that his ideas about the indispensability of free competition among all kinds of institutions—businesses, voluntary organizations and governments—are for the first time ever now sweeping across the world with gale force, and radically reshaping the way everyone thinks about how to solve all kinds of problems.

Few today, for example, would argue that competition is not the most effective mechanism to produce efficiency. Few today would argue that a free economy is not the best guarantor of the greatest production of the most desired goods at the lowest possible prices. Few today would argue that government should regulate economic matters and business decisions except for the purpose of increasing competition, ensuring minimal standards of honesty and ethical business behavior, and protecting society from unwarranted externalities.

Government regulation is now taken by most people to be a matter of last, not first, resort.

Those who are concerned with solving problems affecting the public no longer think first about government solutions. Increasingly, they think about which combination of the sectors—public, private, for-profit, and private, not-for-profit—and in what configuration, is best adapted to solving the problem at hand. In other words, thanks to Adam Smith and his successors, we have now started comprehending public problem-solving trisectorally. We now think of government as the last resort, as a partner with other sectors rather than as the sole actor, and with government's role as one of unleashing the power of the two private sectors, helping to facilitate the natural flow of those enormous energies in ways of *their* choosing rather than directing those energies to act in the way of government's choosing. Privatization of public services, contracting out of functions, trisectoral partnerships, leveraging of sectoral strengths, priming markets so as to enable them to work on public problems—these are all ideas that grow directly out of Adam Smith's brilliant formulation of social, economic, and political behavior. And they are winning the world for freedom, efficiency, and greater individual demand-satisfaction, as well as personal fulfillment.

Now all these changes are occurring with great rapidity. Twenty years ago, perhaps even ten years ago, today's consensus did not yet exist. Indeed, it was only eight years ago that the Berlin Wall was toppled by the growing momentum of Adam Smith's revolutionary ideas, sweeping away the frozen, closed, stifling system of Communist command societies that had been imposed on Eastern Europe and the former Soviet Union some seventy years earlier. Why now? Because the pervasiveness of television and other forms of telecommunications across the entire world has enabled nearly everyone everywhere to see and know the benefits of free systems, and to be emboldened by the possibilities they see to throw off the shackles that bind them. For the first time in history, those enslaved in one country can know that there are other, freer ways of organizing societies, and that things do not have to be the way their oppressors make them.

In a time of such rapid change, it is absolutely essential, if one is to keep one's balance, stability, and sense of direction, to remain focused on a few constants that are of enduring relevance and usefulness. One of them—perhaps the most important if society is to continue to evolve in the right direction—is leadership. While command societies permit only one leader, in free societies leadership is in incessant demand because it is utterly indispensable to the functioning of societies with many power centers and literally countless legitimate centers of initiative. It is so obvious a fact, too, that we sometimes miss it. Leadership is indispensable because organizations—organizations of every kind—can act in a unified fashion *only* through leaders. A polity—a community, nation, or state—can act *only* through an authoritative leader.

Leadership is as indispensable to democracy as is the bedrock of popular decision itself. Democracy without leadership is chaos, not unlike the Genesis description of the world as an undifferentiated seething mass. The interaction between proposing, vision-describing, standard-setting leaders, on the one hand, and followers who emulate, challenge, and choose among proposed alternatives, is the essence of democracy.

And when the polity—or the university or corporation—is made up of people who disagree with one another and who distrust one another, it is only a leader trusted by all sides who can enable it to come together, overcome its differences, and speak with one voice, act with one purpose.

Leadership is not praiseworthy unless its primary goal is to serve others. Unredeemed by a value higher than itself, it is simply another form of ego-driven power-seeking. As Aldous Huxley observed, "Idealism is the noble toga that political gentlemen drape over their will to power." We all enjoy the spotlight, but those who seek it primarily, rather than the preceding accomplishment the spotlight is meant to honor, are self-serving to the core. Honor, attention, glory can properly follow achievement, but cannot, without vitiating the character of the leader, be the goals themselves. As the poet John Ruskin observed, "The highest reward for a person's toil is not what he gets for it but what he becomes through it." Or as Shakespeare's Duke Vincentio says in *Measure for Measure*:

> Heaven doth with us as we with torches do,
> Not light them for themselves; for if our virtues
> Did not go forth of us, 'twere all alike
> As if we had them not.

That idea is captured beautifully in the Bible. The Hebrew word for leader—prince or king—is the same as that for clouds, which draw up moisture from the oceans and seas only for the purpose of sprinkling it back on the land as rain. The clouds exist—as the prince or leader exists—for the good of those whom they benefit.

To be effective, leaders must inspire trust. None of us will follow anyone whom we don't trust. And if we do trust someone, we will follow him or her in hard times as well as good. Trust is the indispensable ingredient in enabling us to face the sacrifices that are often part of any institution's life, whether a corporation, a university or a nation. The primary problem in our public life today is a lack of trust. Leaders lie to the public to get elected and pander to the voters to stay in office. Why should anyone willingly pay more in taxes if he or she doesn't trust the government to do what it promises in order to gain agreement for those taxes? Compulsive poll-taking political leaders in this age of television politics remind me of Robespierre, the leader of the French revolutionaries two centuries ago, who said: "The crowd is in the streets. I must see where they are going because I am their leader."

Leaders who are trusted will be given leeway to lead more boldly and to chart longer-term courses. Because we trust them to choose the course that will benefit us, we take their word that, whatever the sacrifices they say we must endure, we will benefit down the road if we follow their vision. We follow because we trust.

How do leaders gain the trust of their institutions and followers?

They tell the truth, and demand the same of others.

They say what they think, and insist that others follow suit. They struggle to avoid saying simply what they think others want to hear.

They work constantly at knowing their institutions down to the tiniest detail, but they don't seek to run it down to the tiniest detail. True leaders know their followers, and they know them personally.

Leaders don't micromanage. They create the circumstances and the frameworks in which their followers can take the initiative. Leadership is an evocative art. Leaders seek to inspire their followers to take the initiative. Leaders orchestrate the evoked energies of others; they set forth a vision and a framework and guidelines but they do not dictate how their followers implement that vision in detail. To do so would be to lose the indispensable advantages of a free institution. A leader is more like an orchestra conductor than a one-man band.

Leaders are not born; they are by-and-large self-made. To lead well, it takes extraordinary humility, unlimited self-control, self-mastery, self-discipline, and ego-restraint.

Leaders seek to renew their institutions and are most concerned with self-renewal of their followers. Leaders seek to surround themselves with others who are smarter than they are.

It is only through leaders that followers can act and speak at the fullest level of their potential. Leaders need followers in order to realize their visions. Followers need leaders in order to provide a framework for their energies and initiative in particular directions. True leaders will always be mindful that the achievement which they are ever-tempted to regard as solely their own is in reality the result of the miracle of reciprocal support of followers for their leadership. Winston Churchill put it best, as he usually did with everything. At some grand occasion celebrating his eightieth birthday, Clement Attlee introduced him as "the man whose lion's heart had saved England in World War II." When Churchill took the podium, he began as follows: "May I correct my honorable colleague and friend. It was the people of this Island of ours who were the heart of the lion. I had the great good luck to be the lion's ROAR." I cannot resist the temptation to note that it was that same Attlee whom Churchill years before had described as a sheep in sheep's clothing. It would seem that, at age eighty, the lion can indeed lie down with the lamb.

To be the leader of a university is both easier and harder than leading other kinds of institutions. It is easier because there is general agreement across all constituencies that the basic purposes of the institution are to advance knowledge that is likely to benefit humanity, to transmit knowledge and skills from one generation to the next, and to serve the communities in which it is located. It is harder because, as one president put it, being president of a university is like presiding over a cemetery. The president is above everyone but no one listens. Unlike a corporate CEO or the commander-in-chief of a nation, university presidents cannot command their most important constituencies—faculty and students—to do anything. Their only asset is moral suasion. If they are moral exemplars in their personal lives and moral beacons in their vision for their universities, they can move mountains even without the power to command them to move, indeed even more effectively than if they had such power.

That is the kind of president Sam Cook has been for Dillard University. When he assumed the presidency a quarter of a century ago, he had a vision of what Dillard had the potential of being. It was a vision of a Dillard with significantly higher academic achievement, with better and more highly trained faculty, with a larger number of graduates going on to the best graduate and professional schools in the nation, with a larger number of graduates better equipped for challenging careers in all kinds of business, especially in technology-based industries, with outreach to other nations in the world, with greater service to New Orleans and the state of Louisiana, with an alumni body that would be more deeply involved in, as well as more generously supportive of, alma mater, with national stature in some fields of activity, and with the habit of producing graduates who could write, speak, and serve society at the highest level of students from any institution in the nation.

Sam Cook realized that vision. To succeed in doing so required that he articulate it clearly, repeat it frequently, and fight, cajole, and persist in seeing it through to realization. He could do so only because of his extraordinary leadership talents. He is animated not by ego, but by an ideal of service to an institution. He is animated not by elitist aspirations, but by an insistence that only the highest possible standards of quality are appropriate for his faculty and his students, not for his sake but for theirs. Like any great leader, and Sam Cook is surely great by anyone's standards, he believed in his heart of hearts that Dillard had the potential to be much greater than its faculty and students thought at any given point in time. He saw a Dillard as it could be rather than as it was. He saw the Dillard of the future, not the past or the present.

And he succeeded in leading Dillard from that past and present into a future of his envisioning because he earned the trust of his faculty, administration, students, alumni, and community. Some came along reluctantly at first, but very soon all came along with enthusiasm. By the second decade of his presidency, he could do no wrong. And even then, he was not tempted to rest on his laurels, to glory in his achievement, to indulge himself in self-satisfaction. He simply redoubled his efforts, set his sights for Dillard ever higher, and brought everyone to a continuously higher plane of performance.

Vision, ideals, standards, toughness, persistence, courage, and trustworthiness. Those are the qualities which any leader needs to be effective, and they are what enabled Sam Cook to create a legacy at Dillard that is the envy of all institutions of higher education. The nation desperately needs more leaders like Sam Cook, and one can only hope that others will be inspired by, as well as learn from, his truly remarkable achievements at Dillard University.

10

Homage to the Brave

Leslie Dunbar

As friends do when one of their number dies, I phoned Sam Cook on the evening Martin Luther King Jr. was assassinated. Sam had known Martin better than I. They had been classmates at Morehouse, and their friendship had continued. It seems fitting, therefore, that my contribution to this *festschrift* for this man I so greatly respect and cherish be words I spoke about Dr. King as an address on Martin Luther King Day in 1995 at my Durham church. That it was a Baptist church may be appropriate, too, for this longtime leader of a United Methodist university, who closes his *Who's Who* entry with these two words: "Democrat, Baptist."

The nation has made of Dr. King's birthday a national holiday. Why, though do we of the church specially honor him? Most church bodies do not have a Washington, Jefferson, Lincoln Sunday. Why a Martin Luther King Sunday?

I think the answer could only be that the church acknowledges him as a successor to those prophets of old who pronounced judgments and then set before the people the path to redemption, to recovery of God's favor.

Like all persons I have known or know about, King had done some things he probably should not have done. Like many if not all of us, he may have violated one or more of the Ten Commandments.

But—and this is more important—there was one commandment he did obey consistently. It was the first: "You must have no other gods beside me." That may be the most widely disobeyed of all the Ten Commandments.

King's public career was short: from 1955 to his murder by an assassin's gun in 1968. To my observation, throughout those thirteen years he served no other god: not the god of racial pride or supremacy; not the god of state power; not the god of communism, socialism, capitalism, or any other ideological "ism."

Baptists are committed to living in total personal responsibility to God, with nothing between them and the divine presence, or shielding them from it. An old Tom T. Hall song says it in a way that could almost be a Baptist theme song—that Jesus and the believer have it all worked out and don't need anybody to tell them what it's all about. It takes courage to assume such unshielded responsibility. King was a Baptist.

I chaired a meeting, as was my occasional role, of leaders of the civil rights movement on Sunday, April 16, 1967. It was a tense time. The country was locked into its war in Vietnam. King had begun to speak strongly against it. His most forceful statement had been in an address just twelve days earlier at New York's Riverside Church.

For his stand he was being widely criticized by our government, by leading newspapers, and by some other leaders of the civil rights movement. They thought the war and civil rights should be kept separate. On the day before our meeting at a New York hotel, King had been in an antiwar march in Manhattan.

Our meeting (one product of which, incidentally, was the creation of the forerunner of the Children's Defense Fund) began in midmorning, then continued through lunch. As convener and chair, I had brought up the rear as we walked into the hotel's dining room, with King and an equally eminent leader, one of his strongest critics, alongside him. I have never forgotten the brief interchange between them:

"Martin, I see in the papers that you were marching yesterday."

And then King, in that voice that always seemed to come from heaven's own choir, responded, "Yes, Roy, and where were you?"

"Where were you?" That's a prophet's question. It is also a question a proper preacher could challenge his listeners with. Not I. I've enough trouble asking myself, "Where was I?" for all those too-many times when I had not the will or the courage to act as circumstances required. I have not the right to ask another, "Where were you?"

During the last three or four years of King's life, his message broadened and deepened. Earlier years had been absorbed in the southern struggle against discrimination and segregation. After 1965, he spoke more directly against poverty. He was, when killed, organizing the Poor Peoples' March on Washington, which then went on, though somewhat lamely, in 1968 without him.

There was yet more. In his last year, he was passionately speaking against war. First of all, the war against Vietnam, but beyond that, revulsion over all war and militarism.

King knew what his newer preaching meant; two days before our New York meeting he had said, in a speech at Stanford University: "I'm convinced that many of the very people who supported us in the struggle in the South are not willing to go all the way now," (as quoted by David J. Garrow in *Bearing the Cross* [William Morrow, 1986]: 712).

The present fact is that they—we—have mostly forgotten what he was saying those last months.

In all the near-endless remembrance about his "dream," what will be said about his indictment of our economic system for its perpetuation of poverty?

What will be said about his confrontation with our military culture?

It is wrong to declare what someone now dead would be thinking and doing if alive. We nevertheless can wonder. For myself, I can't believe King would be abandoning old causes. He had, and I borrow Langston Hughes's fine words,

Plowed a new furrow
Across the field of history.

And he always had known to:

Keep your hand on the plow.
Hold on.

The witness of his last years is that he would be a determined enemy of whatever, worldwide, keeps the poor, and of whatever keeps nations in arms and at war.

This was the King the church must, it seems to me, recognize and honor.

The Book of Deuteronomy tells us that the word of God "is very near to you," "not in the heavens" but "on your lips and in your heart ready to be kept" (30:9–16). Our friend Jim Crenshaw has slightly reworded this:

> The will of God is not far off, so that you would have to search for it in high heaven or beyond the sea. Instead, it confronts you as a gift, very near to you. Life is present, in your heart, and you *can* keep God's commands.

And that requires a lot of asking, "Where was I?"

It takes a lot of courage to believe that we, each of us, without the assistance of priest or dogma, walk around with God's word in our hearts and minds. Perhaps too it takes arrogance. We are reminded that there is often a thin line cleaving our nature. There is also tension between the Baptist insistence on separation of church and state and our obedience to that prophetic tradition which orders us to speak for the poor and for peace.

This passage from Deuteronomy was quoted by Paul in the Epistle to the Romans (10:8). The Gospel of Luke also quotes from the Old Testament, from the Book of Isaiah. Two great messages, and ones that help to link Jews and Christians in brotherhood and common fealty.

According to Luke, Jesus began his ministry by reading from Isaiah:

> The Spirit of the Lord is upon me, because he has anointed me to bring good news to the poor. He has sent me to proclaim release to the captives and recovery of sight to the blind.

This was his opening announcement. This was what he said would be his ministry, his program (and not a word in it about middle-class tax relief!). This is the platform from which he never departed. If we are going to bother to call ourselves his church, I think it must be our platform.

It was King's. He witnessed for it in the street, and for it he time and again went to jail. I sometimes wonder if the people, including many of our political leaders, who annually recall his "I Have a Dream" speech of 1963 also remember that he repeatedly tested our laws and went to jail and led his followers to jail. Willie Nelson has a song about Jesus called "The Troublemaker." That was King, too: a dreamer, yes, but his dream led him to be a troublemaker, a disturber of the peace, all over the South, and elsewhere, too.

Prophets seldom succeed, at least in their own times. Did any of the Old Testament prophets change their rulers, their own societies? The prophet Nathan did reduce King David to sackcloth and ashes, but we don't read that much good was thereby accomplished. Did North Carolina's celebrated son, Paul Green, achieve any victories by his lonesome vigils outside Central Prison when executions were to take place?

"To kill a man in judicial cold blood," he wrote in 1945 to the then-governor, "is but to deny any possible development and amelioration in that man's character."

Prophets seldom win, in their time. King probably did, more often than most. As we today see the curse of drugs, crime, and poverty on our land, we may see ourselves as faithless stewards of his achievements. Luke tells us that after Jesus began his ministry by reading those words—"announce good news to the poor, proclaim release for the prisoners"—that among his listeners, who were his fellows townspeople, "there was general approval"—they were astonished that "words of such grace should fall from his lips." But when he continued and told them that God might sometime set the needs of foreigners ahead of theirs, the "congregation was roused to fury." They chased him out of town.

Some of us rate King's "Letter from Birmingham Jail" as the strongest of his writings. Eight Alabama clergymen had by public statement rebuked him for leading a mass demonstration at that particular time in Birmingham. From his jail cell he responded to these Protestant, Roman Catholic, and Jewish clergymen. The "Letter" may consequently be considered as an epistle to the church.

At one place in it he remarked that although it was not uncommon for ministerial associations and other church bodies to release statements calling on southerners to comply peacefully with the federal courts' desegregation decisions, he had not yet—this was 1963—seen a statement by them saying that segregation was wrong, that "integration is morally right—because the Negro is your brother."

A short time before, however, and probably unnoticed yet by King, out in Mississippi twenty-eight young Methodist ministers had done just what he called for, in a public statement.

"The Church," they had said, "is the instrument of God's purpose. This is His Church. It is ours only as stewards under His Lordship." Then quoting the Methodist *Discipline*, they continued, "Our Lord Jesus Christ teaches that all men are brothers. He permits no discrimination because of race, color, or creed. 'In Christ Jesus you are all sons of God, through faith.'" A Methodist minister "champions justice, mercy, freedom, brotherhood, and peace. He defends the underprivileged, oppressed, and forsaken. He challenges the status quo, calling for repentance and change whenever the behavior of men falls short of the standards of Jesus Christ."

When we meet to honor Martin Luther King Jr., I have constantly to remind myself that he was dead and buried before most of today's college students were born, and that others were too young to be much aware. For those who blessedly are so young, it may be hard to believe that this statement of these twenty-eight Methodist preachers was an act of rare bravery. So mindful had they been of its risks, that they had carefully screened out all possible signers except native Mississippians.

In about a year's time, all twenty-eight were forced out of their pulpits and out of Mississippi. This happened despite the authority a Methodist bishop can exert. What a price the church was willing to pay, driving from a state as small as Mississippi twenty-eight of its finest young clergy, in order to enforce a secular ideology, in order to serve "another god." What a difference there might have been in that state in the following years had those brave persons been allowed to do their work.

All of us who can remember those years know that the fault was not only that of our Methodist brethren. In the flush days of the War on Poverty of the 1960s and 1970s, it used to be joked that the many agencies set up by that so-called war (which never amounted to more than guerrilla skirmishes) were staffed mostly by preachers who had been too bold for their congregations. Not true, but not altogether wrong. Some of them I knew, and they included Baptists.

Baptists have no bishops to make their decisions for them. Each of our congregations has to be brave, all by itself. Each has to choose to whom and to what to be faithful. King is so impressive to me because of his brave and unswerving commitment to that first commandment: "You must have no other gods beside me."

Those courageous young Mississippi preachers had, nevertheless, felt it necessary to conclude their statement by bowing before the popular insistence on a political virtue: "We affirm," they said, "an unflinching opposition to Communism." Why had they to say that, except that our secular society required it, out of conformity? King was a freer person.

The true meaning of courage is simply this, to do one's job: to fulfill your job's obligations. King throughout his thirteen years of public leadership was "doing his job," the job of one claiming to be called by God.

We Baptists make the claim that we need no priest, that we in our congregations can hear and heed God's will. We are committed to the faith that the word is "very near," is not out of our reach.

We are religious democrats. In our democratic political nation we claim that we can define justice, can know it. The question is, do we define justice, do we apply justice, in a way approved by God?

There is widespread concern today with moral values and whether we are losing them. In his great Riverside Church speech of 1967, King had this to say:

A true revolution of value will soon cause us to question the fairness and justice of many of our past and present policies. On the one hand we are called to play the Good Samaritan on life's roadside; but that will be only an initial act. One day we must come to see that the whole Jericho Road must be transformed so that men and women will not be constantly beaten and robbed as they make their journey on Life's highway. . . . A true revolution of values will soon look uneasily on the glaring contrast of poverty and wealth. . . . A true revolution of values will lay hands on the world and say of war, "This way of settling differences is not just."

Courage is doing one's job: do the job you accept.

The courage required of King was to do what he was called to do, to pastor, to lead, to speak truth to power. We honor him for his faithfulness.

If that mystic metaphor which calls the church the "body of Christ" has meaning for us, then the courage of a bishop, or the courage of a congregation, is to protect the church, is to be faithful to its mission. It seems to me that a congregation manifests its courage when it is true to Jesus' first summons, and thus wants to serve the poor and the afflicted. "Today," says the Scripture, "I offer you the choice of life and good, or death and evil. . . . Choose life and you and your descendants will live; love the Lord your God, obey him, and hold fast to him; that is life for you" (Deut. 30:15, 19).

King closed any number of his speeches by declaiming with the prophet Amos, "let justice flow on like a river and righteousness like a never-failing torrent." We in his years would listen to him, would hear him, and would allow ourselves to believe it was possible, that such a time might be.

Those assassins' guns, and wars abroad, and division of our people here withered those hopes, took away much of our belief in their possibility.

But as long as we may be a true church, as long as we have the courage to "have no other gods," that hope that King raised, the hope that we could here create a society which truly chooses life, over death, that hope can still live.

11

What Are You Doing for Others?

Johnnetta B. Cole

Like every man, every woman must decide whether she will walk in the light of creative altruism or the darkness of destructive selfishness. This is the judgement. Life's most persistent and urgent question is, what are you doing for others?

With these words, Dr. Martin Luther King Jr. confronts us with a serious question, cast in powerfully simple language, "What are you doing for others?"

Dillard sisters and brothers, what are you doing for others? Some folks will quickly answer: "Why, I'm leading them, that's what I'm doing for them. I'm in the business of leadership!"

Then let me ask, what is leadership? Let me ask, where are our leaders? Let me ask again, what are you doing for others?

The *Oxford English Dictionary* defines leadership as: "deserved influence, to motivate, encourage, guide and direct the movements of men, women and institutions."

If this is leadership, then we are pitifully short of it these days. How desperately we look for those who are filled with personal integrity and wisdom, and we search for those who have the creativity and dedication to serve others, the ability to inspire us.

The decline of visible leaders over the past decade has not been limited to the political ranks. Scandal has discredited boardrooms, school boards, and pulpits. And in recent years, the decline in leadership was accompanied by a rise in what has been labeled the yuppies and buppies—young urban professionals and the black version. Taken in the best and most positive sense, these young professionals may be seen as educated, capable individuals who work hard and, therefore, deserve to enjoy the fruits of their labor. There is nothing wrong with this. Do we not all strive to receive that which we have worked for—to enjoy the fruits of a good life? But in their most negative manifestation, yuppies and buppies are greedy, self-centered individuals who place profit and personal privileges above progress, laws, or morality. Such behavior is deeply alarming because it stunts the growth of the individual and it certainly prevents the development of a community.

We do not envy individual success, but we must constantly decide what success is and how we can measure it. That great teacher, Dr. King, once said, "We are prone to judge success by the index of our salaries or the size of our automobiles, rather than by the quality of our service and relationship to humanity."

Those of us who do "succeed" must remember that the freedoms and protections that enable us to study, work, and achieve are the fruits of the labor of so many other folks. If you get there—to success that is—you will not have gotten there on your own.

Despite popular belief, there are few *born* leaders. Quality leadership is learned and it is earned. We cannot expect Dillard women and men to acquire leadership skills by some process of osmosis. There must be deliberate steps to *educate* for leadership. We must teach, best of all by example, my colleagues—we must teach that leadership is, at its very core, service to others.

Harriet Tubman wasn't a leader because she struggled and fought for her own freedom. Harriet Tubman was a leader because she risked her own freedom a million times so that others could gain theirs.

Mary McLeod Bethune wasn't a leader because she sacrificed and struggled for her own education. Mary McLeod Bethune was a leader because she dreamed and planned and worked for the education of others.

Marian Wright Edelman isn't a Spelman alumna who is a leader because she cares about and works in defense of her own children. Although to do so is to be human. Marian Wright Edelman is a leader because she fights for the rights of all children.

Nelson Mandela isn't a leader because he confronts and challenges apartheid in the interest of his own dignity. Nelson Mandela is a leader because his efforts and his sacrifices are for the basic human rights of a people.

Dillard sisters and brothers, you too can be leaders, indeed you can be great. As Dr. King taught us:

> Everybody can be great because anybody can serve. You don't have to have a college degree to serve. You don't have to make your subject and verb agree to serve. You don't have to know about Plato and Aristotle to serve. You don't have to know Einstein's theory of relativity to serve. You don't have to know the second theory of thermodynamics in physics to serve. You only need a heart full of grace. A soul generated by love.

I deeply fear what happens when we have a group of people who indeed know so much, but do so little. Think about our country where we know how to send people to the moon, but seem not to care that millions of Americans must see that moon every night, as they sleep in the full discomfort of their homelessness. We are a society that knows how to run almost everything by a machine. But we seem to have lost our intelligence, our ability to figure out how to stop some folks from discriminating against other folks.

I am profoundly frightened by a society where there are people who know so much but do so little for others. As Langston Hughes put it, "We have got lots of folks who are colleged, but too few who are educated."

There are polls and studies which suggest that we may be coming out of the period where students want to do everything for themselves but nothing for others. Could it be that the long lean years of "meism" are drawing to an end? Could it be that we are seeing the last of an era when social responsibility became old-fashioned and service for others was what you said you would do after you made a million dollars for yourself?

Let us hope that we are returning to a sense of leadership as service. Tell me, Dillard sisters and brothers, when you dream about your future, is that dream about more than a closet full of fine clothes, and a garage filled with a fancy car or two? Can you also dream of the sheer joy of spending Saturday afternoons at a Y tutoring little brothers and sisters? When you imagine yourself as a $60,000-a-year professional, do you also think about how much of that you might be able to give to projects, organizations, causes that address those who will not see $60,000 in their lifetime?

Think about our country and our people and how much needs to be done. In 1989, in one of the wealthiest and most technologically advanced nations in the world, these conditions prevailed and have changed little since then:

More than one-third of all black Americans and nearly one-third of Hispanic Americans were living in poverty.

On average, black families earned only 56 percent of what their white counterparts earned. Unemployment for black men was more than twice what it was for white men (12.7 percent and 5.4 percent). There were more black men in prisons than in colleges and universities. Black youth age 18–19 with a high school diploma had an unemployment rate of 40.6 percent; those 20–24 years old with a high school diploma, an unemployment rate of 26.7 percent. Black women headed 41.5 percent of all black households in America.

And when we focus in on our children, on black children, listen to the following frightening figures. In comparison to white children black children are twice as likely to die in the first year of life, see a parent die, or live in substandard housing.

In comparison with white children, black children are three times as likely to be poor and die of child abuse.

In comparison with white children, black children are four times as likely to be murdered before one year of age or as a teenager, or be incarcerated between fifteen and nineteen years of age.

In comparison with white children, black children are five times more likely to be dependent on welfare.

Dillard sisters and brothers, you along with your counterparts in every one of our historically black colleges and universities must build steady bridges into the communities of the poor or you will drown in your selfishness and inaction.

You see, there is no hiding place from the crises and disasters or our times.

Drugs are all over our cities; violence appears in "good" neighborhoods just as in "bad" ones, and poverty now affects increasing numbers of folks who used to be working class if not middle class.

Each of us is affected by the destruction of the very fiber of our society that follows from babies having babies, irrational violence, and widespread dependence on drugs and alcohol.

Each of us must learn to act in whatever ways we can to save others—to save ourselves.

I'm not so naive as to think that the profoundly serious problems of our country will be solved by the actions of individuals alone. I'm realistic enough to know that we must demand that our government do its part to address the problems of our children, our elderly, the homeless, and the poor. We must also entice the business community to carry out its responsibility to share some of what it has accumulated. And the philanthropic community must continue to give—indeed give even more in the interest of a stronger and healthier nation.

But, in addition to what must be done by these sectors, elected officials and organizations and philanthropic groups—in short by effective laws, well-designed and managed programs, and generous gifts—in addition to all of this, there is a role for each of us. As Dr. King put it:

All too many of us who live in affluent America ignore those who exist in poor America; in doing so, the affluent Americans will eventually have to face themselves with the question that Eichmann chose to ignore: How responsible am I for the well-being of my fellows? To ignore evil is to become an accomplice to it.

There is a new feeling afoot in the U.S. as Americans seem to be rediscovering doing for others. As you know, there have been many different bills in Congress calling for national service and community involvement by our young and not-so-young folks. Why, the president of the U.S. has called on us to let our little lights shine.

I cannot argue here the merits of these various bills, although I can't resist saying that we must be careful not to let a decent and meaningful idea—community service—rest on a system of haves and have-nots, so that the poor do service among the poor and the rich do what they please.

Finally then, let me pose the question, how can you learn to serve? I think the easiest way to become involved is to become aware. Open your eyes and ears and soul to the conditions of our people. But I also think that there is something to be said for the approach of some high schools and colleges which today require a certain number of hours of community service for graduation.

Once you incorporate service into your life, you realize that it is in fact a rewarding way to live. As Dr. King once said:

> An individual has not started living until he can rise above the narrow confines of his individualistic concerns to the broader concerns of all humanity.

Let me draw closure now and call for you here at this great university and indeed throughout the colleges and universities of our nation to serve others. And it is a double call to honors students—because from you we expect the most and the best.

Let me end as I began, with the words of a man who truly served others:

> Like every man, every woman must decide whether she will walk in the light of creative altruism or the darkness of destructive selfishness. This is the judgement. Life's most persistent and urgent question is, what are you doing for others?

Brother president, as you bring closure on a sterling presidency at Dillard, I wish the very best for you and my Spelman sister Sylvia. And may your daughter, Karen, and your son, Dubie, continue to make a reality of our people's saying: "Apple don't fall far from the tree."

12

Academic Moralist

Julius S. Scott Jr.

I am pleased and deeply honored to be asked by Tom Trotter to contribute to this *festschrift*. Samuel DuBois Cook and I go way back. We have a common mentor, the inimitable Dr. Benjamin Elijah Mays. We share a common mission and vocation, and we are ideological partners. We began college presidencies on the same day, January 1, 1975, and we have been close colleagues.

It has been an inspiration to hear his clarion voice and experience his singular impact in denominational and professional educational circles related to quality higher education.

Any recognition of the contributions of Sam Cook must take into account his deep insights into the nature and being of higher learning. My assessment is that chief among his contributions to the thrust of the enterprise of learning is his resolute and formidable embodiment of its quintessential moral quality. I dub him the academic moralist, and this brief piece celebrates that genius.

What are the elements of Cook's academic moralism? First, he understands the character of knowledge and the nature of higher learning to be metaphysical, ultimate. "Ontological" is the term he delights to use; i.e., knowledge for him has to do with transcendent, eternal verities (Cook's epistemology). His posture is ontological, and he visualizes this ontology as fundamental.

Upon the announcement of his appointment to the presidency of Dillard University, he said, "I come . . . as one who worships at the altar of the goddess of truth, inquiry, knowledge, and wisdom, as one committed to the creative and redemptive character of life of the mind" (address to the Dillard faculty, March 22, 1974). And in an excellent paper, he asserts, "the separation of education and morality is fraught with all kinds of dangers and terrible consequences, as Nazi Germany demonstrated with utter clarity and horror." (Remaining quotes, unless otherwise noted, from Cook, "The Wisdom de Profundis of Benjamin E. Mays, Black Colleges, and the Good Life" [*Quarterly Review*, summer 1995]: 123–37 passim.)

And in that same monograph, he affirms:

The love of truth is an expression of the love of God, and the search for truth is a rational and experimental inquiry into the order and laws of nature and God.

His tenures on the University Senate and the Council of Presidents of The United Methodist Church have been marked by continuously calling the institutions and the chief executive officers to awareness of the moral nature of their raison d'etre.

The second element of Cook's academic moralism has to do with his theory of educational values (his axiology). The content and context for learning are inexorably, "intrinsically, and instrumentally value-laden."

He sees values as primordial:

Institutions of higher education must recapture their unique moral and ethical foundations, authority, resources, influence, and creative power in order to improve the quality of life and the content of character in the body politic and commonwealth.

Colleges and universities must be concerned with and involved in the pursuit of values in the discharge of their missions. No value neutrality here; no dispassionate objectivity here!

Colleges and universities have an obligation to nurture and foster humanistic education concerned with the common good . . . education must be committed to improving the quality of life for all members of the society, and especially the most needy, the most vulnerable, the weak, the disinherited, the poor, the exploited, the oppressed, the downtrodden, the victims of injustice, degradation, discrimination, and dehumanization.

Cook's view of higher learning is that institutions must eschew negative and dysfunctional values, such as intolerance, "complacency, mediocrity, low aims, and self-satisfaction." And:

Indeterminate higher possibilities beckon and drive us. . . . In every achievement, the voice of higher possibility calls to move us on to another level and plateau, greater heights and peaks.

Social change is a major value of higher education. Historically black colleges and universities are superbly qualified to take leadership in values related to the integration of the races. These institutions are the "crowning glory of life of the mind—not the White or the Black mind . . . but life of the mind."

The social relevance of education is for Cook akin to Martin Luther King Jr.'s "beloved community," which Cook defines as

the creation of a society of human brotherhood and equality—recognizing the solidarity of all mankind, the healing of wounds, the binding of torn social tissues, the making of this land one people, whole, unified, free, humane, equal. (address to the Dillard faculty, March 22, 1974)

The creation at Dillard of the only National Center for Black-Jewish Relations sprang from Cook's conviction that the university must be about the embodiment of the values of the "beloved community."

The third facet of Cook's academic moralism is his insistence that at the heart of higher learning are purpose and meaning (teleology).

Education has an end, a destiny. This teleology, this discourse of ends, was affirmed by Cook at the first meeting of the faculty upon his assuming the presidency of Dillard. "Dillard does have a call from history," he affirmed, "and a date with destiny."

In the essay on Dr. Mays, he challenged his colleagues to emulate Mays's commitment to higher learning and his sense of teleology by grasping the goals and destiny of education as "motive, norm, source, ground, meaning, end, and fulfillment of human existence."

Sam Cook has painted the texture of academic moralism in rich, deep, and indelible colors. His enormous embodiment of the nature and urgency of the moral quality of higher learning will have abiding impact and puts a challenge before us all.

Thanks, Sam!

13

We Remember with Pride

Jamye Coleman Williams and McDonald Williams

Life offers us many rewarding experiences—none more important than developing lifelong friendships. On this occasion of your retirement from the presidency of Dillard University, we remember with pride your many contributions to the academic arena and with gratitude our friendship for more than forty years.

Our paths first crossed when all of us were graduate students at Ohio State University. In those days, black students were not as numerous on predominately white college and university campuses as they are today. It was, therefore, not unusual to know many of your peers, even though you were not in the same discipline. Your discipline was political science; Mac's, English; and Jamye's, speech communication. Regardless, we shared the harried life of the graduate student: endless classroom preparation, study in the stacks and the carrels, term papers, final exams, the dissertation, general examinations, the final oral. Yet this was not without relief as we socialized over meals at Pomerene Hall or the student union, visited Long's Bookstore, or sat in Ohio Stadium to witness the traditional rivalry on the gridiron between the Michigan Wolverines and the Ohio State Buckeyes.

It was interesting that two years following your and Mac's graduation in 1954 with Ph.D. degrees we found ourselves in Atlanta, with you at Atlanta University and us at Morris Brown College. We remember that one of your major contributions during this period was the Town Hall Meeting forums. Believing that higher education is indispensable to black liberation, you invited outstanding and influential persons of both races to address the problems of the time. This was during the late fifties when civil unrest was beginning to stir. We recall vividly an appearance by Ralph McGill, distinguished editor of the Atlanta *Constitution*, whose candor about the pain of racism is still a part of our memories.

After two years we left Atlanta for Nashville to accept positions at Tennessee State University. We continued, nevertheless, to follow with great interest your ever-developing, distinguished career.

When you were program officer for the Ford Foundation and we chanced to be in New York for a professional meeting, you would awaken us at midnight to engage in a spirited conversation about the world in general and academe in particular. We remember the contributions you made to blacks and other minorities while you were with the foundation. You were an influencing factor in the Ford Foundation's unprecedented commitment of $100 million to minorities.

When you became president of Dillard University, we rejoiced in this significant milestone, believing that the institution would be the better for your leadership. Because of your commitment to justice, we were duly impressed when you established the National Center for Black-Jewish Relations and sponsored national conferences to generate honest dialogue, especially among young people. We applauded your establishment of an endowed Benjamin E. Mays—Samuel DuBois Cook Presidential Scholarship Award to recognize academic achievement, leadership ability, exemplary citizenship, and professional promise.

During your presidency at Dillard, you came to Nashville to an annual meeting of the African-American presidents of United Methodist colleges and universities. In the early years we could expect a call from you at some odd hour, saying you were at the airport en route home. Finally, in exasperation Jamye said to you, "It is later than you think! You'd better start arranging to see us once a year—before it's too late." That admonition must have struck a responsive chord, because we now look forward to sharing some quality time with Sylvia and you when autumn comes around each year.

As Sylvia and you leave Dillard, the responsibility of leading one of the top five schools in the 1995 Best Value in the South category for regional liberal arts colleges, we wish you a retirement filled with rewarding memories. But while you may have retired officially, the world of academe in general and that of Atlanta in particular will be doing itself an injustice should it not continue to draw upon your vast experience in the field of higher education.

We know that you will continue to be restless about the escalating problems that plague our country. We are sure that you will continue to make a difference in the lives you will touch. Your concern about hatred, bigotry, and intolerance will find a response in love, acceptance, and tolerance. Your belief that all of us must possess character and integrity, courage, and compassion, will keep you ever moving toward making the world a better place than you found it.

14

The Main Thing Is not to Be Afraid

David S. Goldstein

The extraordinary contributions to human harmony and goodness which Samuel DuBois Cook has given us are legend in his own lifetime. Anyone who has ever been touched by his spirit knows that. He has forged numerous coalitions of decency by the strength of his amazing mind and will. None is more important than the National Center for Black-Jewish Relations.

His name, Samuel, after the Hebrew prophet, means "he who has heard God." When one considers the life and works of Sam Cook, a number of descriptive adjectives come to mind: vision, courage, dynamite energy, towering intelligence. Truly his heart has been open to hearing God's voice.

I think of another sage who heard God's voice, Rabbi Nahman of Bratzlav, the Hassidic thinker, who once said,

> The whole world is nothing but a very narrow bridge.
> And the main thing is not to be afraid.

There is a story about another very narrow bridge, over which a man was resolved to cross in order to begin at last a life too long wasted and delayed.

The Main Thing Is not to Be Afraid

As he started out across the bridge he saw another person coming from the opposite direction, dressed like him except for a long rope tied around his waist.

They stood face to face. The stranger asked him to hold the end of the rope tightly. He agreed.

Whereupon, and without the slightest warning, the stranger suddenly jumped over the side. The man held fiercely, as the stranger dangled close to oblivion.

"What are you doing?" he shouted.

"I am your responsibility," the stranger called back. "If you let go, I am lost."

"But I can't pull you up alone. You must help. Climb back up the rope," he implored.

Yet as much as he pleaded, the stranger refused.

"In that case," the man at last said, "I return to you the responsibility for your own life."

"How can you be so selfish?" the stranger berated. "What could be so important that you would refuse me?"

The man waited for a while. But the stranger remained as before—unwilling.

"Then I accept your choice," the man said and opened his hands.

That's a story many of us know. There are, of course, many interpretations. But in reflecting on the National Center for Black-Jewish relations, I see all converge into one.

The bridge represents the beginning of change. When we decide: What will we do next? Where will we go next? How will we live next?

The bridge is change. And change is never easy. It threatens the comfortable ways we have always seen ourselves. The ways we have always thought and believed and behaved.

And yet, the bridge is also freedom. It can make the future different from the past. It can be liberating.

If crossed, it can free us.

Free us of ways of feeling that belittle us as we belittle others.

Free us of patterns of thinking and acting that keep us trapped in the past.

Free us of the chains that imprison our spirits and hold back our dreams.

Yes, the bridge is the pathway to change.

But the main thing is not to be afraid.

And the rope? What does it teach?

Perhaps, above all, about burdens and duties and obligations and responsibilities which are very real in most lives.

Many of us have also been handed ropes we never asked for or wanted.

Some we willingly accepted, as Sam Cook accepted his.

Others we had no choice but to accept. And perhaps something inside Sam Cook told him also that he had no choice.

The rope is that which tests us. Tests our strengths, our fortitude. Tests our character, our virtues, our values. Our love for others and for ourselves.

The rope tests our faith.

Sometimes we hold on tenaciously. Sometimes we have no choice but to open our hands and let go.

But Rabbi Nahman reminds us: The main thing is not to be afraid.

And, finally, and most enigmatic: the other who approaches us on the bridge. Who is the stranger who comes to meet us? He looks so much like us.

Could the stranger be us? And we hardly recognize him because he represents the self we never quite achieved? The promises and dreams we never quite fulfilled?

Or, most extraordinarily, perhaps it is our own self who is the stranger. We hand the rope to God because we don't believe in our own capacities; are certain we can't save ourselves from life's seeming inevitabilities. From that which is unfair. Unjust. Unexpected. That our inner strength—our resiliency—is insufficient.

But God calls out to us and urges us to be divine partners. To lift ourselves. We must change ourselves. We must believe in ourselves. We must fly!

And the main thing is not to be afraid.

Not to be afraid of growth and change.

Not to be afraid of the bridges we all must cross.

And the main thing is not to be afraid.

This is the ultimate meaning of the work and legacy of Samuel DuBois Cook. Climbing, helping, changing, believing, and yes, flying. Flying!

And the main thing is not to be afraid.

Contributors

Lerone Bennett Jr. is senior editor of *Ebony* magazine in Chicago.

Johnnetta B. Cole is president of Spelman College, Atlanta.

Leslie Dunbar is former executive director of the Southern Regional Council and former executive director of the Field Foundation and lives in Durham, North Carolina.

Joel L. Fleishman is president of the Atlantic Philanthropic Service Company, Inc., New York City.

David S. Goldstein is rabbi of the Touro Synagogue, New Orleans.

Roger W. Ireson is general secretary of the United Methodist Board of Higher Education and Ministry, Nashville.

Shirley A. R. Lewis is president of Paine College, Augusta, Georgia.

William E. Nelson Jr. is research professor of black studies, professor of political science, and director of the Center for Research and Public Policy, The Ohio State University, Columbus.

Contributors

Terry Sanford is former president of Duke University, former governor of North Carolina, and former U.S. senator from North Carolina.

Julius S. Scott Jr. is president of Wiley College, Marshall, Texas.

Gardner Taylor is retired pastor of Concord Baptist Church, Brooklyn, New York.

Kenneth W. Thompson is director of the White Burkett Miller Center of Public Affairs, the University of Virginia, Charlottesville.

F. Thomas Trotter is former president of Alaska Pacific University and is president of the Foundation for United Methodist Communications, Indian Wells, California.

Hanes Walton Jr. is professor in the Department of Political Science, the University of Michigan, Ann Arbor.

Jamye Coleman Williams is former professor of communications and former head of the Department of Communications at Tennessee State University, Nashville.

McDonald Williams is former professor of English and former director of the university honors program at Tennessee State University, Nashville.